# SOUTHAMPTON'S CHAPEL AREA

# SOUTHAMPTON'S CHAPEL AREA

## *A Hundred Years of the Past*

**DAVE MARDEN**

First Published in Great Britain in 2017 by DB Publishing,
an imprint of JMD Media Ltd

ISBN 978-1-78091-560-9

# CONTENTS

# ACKNOWLEDGEMENTS

Although my own fading memories have helped me recreate Chapel, I am grateful to the Southampton City Archives for their help in providing many of the images shown in this book, without which it would have been a much more difficult task to portray the streets and buildings as they were so long ago. Sadly, many of those photographs show the streets just prior to demolition, giving a much different impression than the happier days when life filled the windows and doorways.

Thanks also to others who have helped, in particular to David Goddard for allowing me the use of images from his extensive collection of pub photographs. Again, so vital in depicting the Chapel scene.

Many other photographs have been passed to me from fellow ex-Chapelites and, apart from my own collection, these have proved invaluable. In some cases I have not been able to trace their origins and I hope not to have infringed anyone's copyright by using them. If so, this has been entirely unintentional and I offer my sincere apologies.

In the course of my researches, the following works have been of assistance:

*Chapel and Northam* by Sheila Jemima
*Southampton's Inns and Taverns* by Tony Gallaher
*The Illustrated History of Southampton's Suburbs* by Jim Brown

# SOUTHAMPTON'S CHAPEL AREA

## *A Hundred Years of the Past*

It is now half a century since the last vestiges of the terrace houses were cleared from the streets of Southampton's Chapel district. The tightly-packed, privately-built houses were typical of many of those in industrial areas up and down the country, where cheap homes with affordable rents gave shelter to industrial workers. In many instances, more than one family, or several generations, shared a house and also the rent. Many took in lodgers, often seamen who just needed temporary accommodation between voyages.

The 1960s saw many local authorities clear away such city centre areas in favour of modern council accommodation and tower blocks built on the outskirts of towns and cities, in the name of 'regeneration'. At the time, this was deemed as necessary to provide decent homes in place of dilapidated buildings that were, by then, well below an acceptable living standard. But, sadly, such action destroyed many communities that had grown over many generations and dispersed them to alien territories.

My personal childhood memories from the 1950s recall buildings well past their best, with most being 100 years old. To most people who can remember it, the Chapel area of Southampton was not exactly a salubrious place, and to the casual visitor in past times it was possibly quite fearsome setting foot there, but I would say strangers were treated more with suspicion than hostility. For those of us that lived in the old neighbourhood, it didn't seem so bad. Chapel was probably no different to the back streets of many towns and cities all over the country before they were swept away in the post-war years.

Perhaps a pub on *every* corner is an overstatement, but there were quite a few. In the area covered by this book there were around seventy, so it is difficult to ignore them as they played a prime role in local life. Almost without exception, every street in the Chapel area had its own pub – some had several, ranging from the elite with polished bars, brass-work and etched mirrors, down to the basic beer house with just a counter and a few sticks of furniture. The grander establishments were fine for relaxation at the weekend. A place to unwind from the week's stress, somewhere to take the wife or girlfriend for an evening of carefree chatter and song, and a place to forget about the workaday problems before the Monday drudgery loomed once more.

The role of the public house around the turn of the 19th century was quite different than that of today. Until World War One there seemed little control over licensing and there was hardly any limit to opening times. Beer was cheap and weak, so a couple of pints were not too much of a strain on brain or pocket. After a hard day's toil and sweat it was necessary to replace the body fluid – sometimes at midday too.

So why write about Chapel? Perhaps because so few others have done so regarding this once proud area that had played such a vital part in Southampton's growth from small town to major city. Historically, Chapel never suffered the terrors, poverty and degradation of the earlier, post-mediaeval slums on the lower and west side of the town; in fact, by comparison it was quite modern, although never very prosperous – at least its inhabitants weren't – but I suspect a few local businessmen and landlords lived quite well off them.

A few years ago, after watching football at St Mary's Stadium, I walked along Melbourne Street, Paget Street, Anglesea Terrace and Albert Road on my way to the Itchen Bridge. It was a journey I had made many times along with thousands of others while mulling over the joys or sorrows of the game that afternoon. At that time the aforementioned streets, and others in the locality, were just a jumble of industrial units, factory depots and weed-strewn lorry parks.

How different all this was from the days when I lived there, and it occurred to me that a great many of my fellow travellers would not have known the old streets as they were in the days when they contained tightly packed houses, shops and pubs, together with the odd local industry. All that had been swept away and almost everything that had existed had now been gone for decades. Chapel, as it was in the old days, now lives in the memories of a diminishing generation of former residents. Not much seems to have been actually written about the area and, consequently, fewer people these days have any idea what was there in the past.

In this book I have attempted to show how the district grew up and to paint a picture of what it was like to live there. The old place changed a great deal during its urban lifetime and, although it was very much past its best in my day, I hope to provide an insight into what was there for more than a century before it disappeared.

I have to admit that in the 1950s and 1960s Chapel had become a grim and tattered place, tired and threadbare after having been gradually run down following the war years and, when the end finally came for the last few rows of houses, it was probably well overdue. It would be very easy to wallow in nostalgia and say what a great place Chapel was, but it certainly wasn't paradise. Everyone over a certain age recalls the hardships of the post-war austerity years but, for all its limitations, life seemed happier then – mainly because you knew no other way. Growing up amongst the tight-knit communities where families had lived together for generations was a fine experience. You didn't just know your neighbours – you knew everyone in your street and most in the ones beyond that – people that were, on the whole, very friendly and generous while, like yourself, being moderately poor and with limited aspirations.

Life certainly seemed much simpler in those days, without the complications and pressures heaped on today's society. Most residents rented their homes from private landlords and very few were self-employed. Mortgages, Council Tax, VAT, luxury consumer goods and designer clothes were all in the future. Families lived day to day and week to week, paid the rent and worried about having enough money left over for life's essentials such as food, fuel and maybe a few pints at the local. Through the eyes of a young child born soon after World War Two, life seemed pretty organised and orderly, and having spent most of my childhood and youth on Chapel's streets I grew up appreciating what little we had and was grateful for the odd (rare) treat.

Over the years, my family lived at three different addresses in Albert Road, and all were much the same with coal fires, a gas cooker and a sink being the basic amenities. The 'garden' was usually a small yard with an outside toilet – not the most welcoming facility on a cold winter night! I still shudder at the thought of the tin bath in front of the open fire, where one side of you got roasted, while the other was frozen by draughts from under the door. We take so many things for granted today, but with no central heating there was often ice *inside* the bedroom windows on cold mornings.

Very few families had a fridge – the nearest thing to that was a meat safe – a cabinet with gauze-covered grilles that kept out the flies. The weekly wash was done in the bath and whites were boiled in a galvanised bucket on the gas stove. To make a phone call you had to walk a street or two to the nearest public box – not that it mattered much, because none of your friends had telephones anyway!

Apart from a pub, many streets also had a local shop. These mainly sold food, cigarettes and confectionary, often on 'tick' (credit) when you could settle up at the end of the week. If you needed anything other than those bare essentials you could always go to Chapel Road, where there were more shops – butchers, bakers, barbers and the like were all on hand – for anything else there were the various emporiums at nearby St Mary Street and East Street.

Apart from a brief spell in London, most of my schooldays were spent in Southampton, firstly at Ascupart Junior (now St Mary's) and then Central Boy's Secondary. These fine institutions turned out generations of pupils that could (mostly) read, write and do sums as an adequate preparation for their future careers, all with a very simple curriculum and without the need of today's league tables, targets and overwhelming assessments. Teachers were given respect – often because they'd hit you if you didn't give it! I suppose it did a lot for discipline but some seemed to derive much pleasure in dishing out such punishment, and some poor individuals seemed always to be on the receiving end.

Growing up was quite exciting. We had lots of adventure playgrounds – they were called bomb sites – where you could explore ruins and cellars, and make camps from the scattered debris. Schoolboy games of the day featured cowboys and indians – and, of course, soldiers. Soapbox carts and pram chassis provided the vehicles for racing around the local streets and over the open ground that had been levelled by the German Air Force. Football, cricket and rounders were all played in back streets that were mainly traffic-free, due to the lack of car owners, as almost everyone used public transport which was cheap and frequent.

Local employment, at least in the 1950s, seemed plentiful, albeit mainly of the low-skilled variety, but there was always work to be had. Wages were low, but then, so were prices, so I suppose it was all relative, and almost everyone seemed to be employed locally in the docks or on the ships that sailed from them. The wharves, factories and shipyards along the River Itchen were also very busy.

So where exactly was Chapel? To me, it was never exactly defined but roughly speaking it was an area between the gasworks to the north and the docks in the south, with the eastern and western boundaries being the River Itchen and the railway line down to the Terminus Station. I have limited this book to those streets that I remember as 'home territory' and if I have omitted places that others consider to be part of Chapel, then I apologise. But I have also included a few streets outside those limits which were part of my childhood and youth.

Without getting too sentimental, I look back and remember Chapel as a decent enough area, with honest and (generally) hard working people, but I'm not so sure I would want to go back to those days, as I'd miss all the comforts of the modern world. However, I do miss the neighbourliness and feeling of community that seems to have evaporated from almost everywhere nowadays. When the bulldozers came, more than just bricks and mortar were removed. The once proud spirit of a bygone era was broken up and scattered around the new housing estates on the edges of town.

In the following pages, I have attempted to recreate the area and streets of old Chapel as they were from the time they were built until the final days as I knew them. Some are now resurrected after so many decades of dereliction and desolation, and those well-worn streets are alive again with smart, modern homes. To the new generation of inhabitants this book may provide an insight into the life that was there in the past, whilst, at the same time, I hope I have stirred some fond memories for the previous occupants.

I have not endeavoured to produce a definitive history about the trials of life from Victorian hardship, the trauma of the Titanic disaster, the horrors through two world wars, and the various economic slumps, but what I have sought to create is a picture of life as it was from the earliest days until its demise around half a century ago, and I trust readers will enjoy this glimpse of the past generations that have walked Chapel's streets.

In order to portray the buildings, people and the general constitution of the area, I have used maps based on Ordnance Surveys, showing the streets in their entirety – that is, prior to World War Two, when so much was obliterated. I trust I will be excused any errors as, over the years, some premises have been renumbered – and even changed address by 'moving' to an adjacent street!

Sadly, Chapel was not a very photogenic place and photographers rarely visited the old streets unless there was a tragedy. The Good, the Bad and the Ugly, Chapel was all of that. Poor people can still be happy. Love and kindness can bring contentment much greater than all the world's riches. By the same token, many wealthy people can be desperately sad. Life's what you make it and in the old days people mainly made the best of a bad job.

Walking down those empty streets and trying to visualise how they were in my boyhood made me aware of how little remains – apart from the memories – and those only live on in people over a certain age. With this in mind, I thought about how I could revive some of those memories in maps and photos and rebuild those streets to let others see what was there so long ago. If this book can do that, it will have achieved its purpose.

Dave Marden 2017

# CHAPTER 1.

## *Chapel – A Brief History*

Before we embark on our tour of Chapel, it is important to know a little of the district's history and how it evolved over its lifetime.

Chapel Road, previously known as Chapel Lane, was once a mediaeval thoroughfare leading from the town to the old Trinity Chapel on the banks of the River Itchen, roughly where Chapel Wharf is today. There was also a tide mill and timber ponds at nearby Crosshouse, from where the ferrymen rowed passengers across the river to the village of Itchen Ferry on the opposite bank.

Shipbuilding at Chapel had become well established by the 1700s and continued until around 1859, while the development of the Baltic Wharf began to establish the area as a commercial quay in the 1830s. Apart from the timber ponds and corn mills the surrounding area was still distinctly rural with fields and meadows, but as other wharves were built (along what is now Marine Parade) traffic increased and the coming of the Floating Bridge in 1836 began the transformation of the district.

The Floating Bridge Company was formed to provide competition with the toll bridge that crossed further up the river at Northam. A new road (Albert Street) was constructed to link the wharves at Marine Parade with the steam ferry to Woolston, creating a shorter route to Portsmouth and, consequently, Chapel Road was now well and truly on the map. With the building of the docks commencing in 1838, and the London & Southampton Railway having been partly operational in 1839, Chapel became what might be described as a 'boom town', and by 1842 streets of terraced houses occupied the previously open land immediately north and south of Chapel Road.

The new expansion consisting of Albert, Paget and Nelson Streets, together with Anglesea and Western Terraces, providing the homes for an army of craftsmen, traders and labourers needed for the many industries associated with the docks, railway and the river, as well as seamen who sailed from the port. The houses were little more than functional, being constructed with poor quality bricks and the walls being clad in slate to stem erosion from the elements. Even so, these were considered somewhat superior to those buildings already in existence. Two downstairs rooms with a scullery, and two bedrooms and a box room above them was the norm, although some buildings offered extra rooms with a third storey or a basement. In the ensuing years, as many as three generations or two families lived together in such tight confines.

The area south of Anglesea Terrace, known as The Marsh, stretched down to the old shoreline (now Canute Road) where the docks had been built, and by 1871 it had also been covered with further terraces including Anderson's, Glebe and Chantry Roads. Ryde

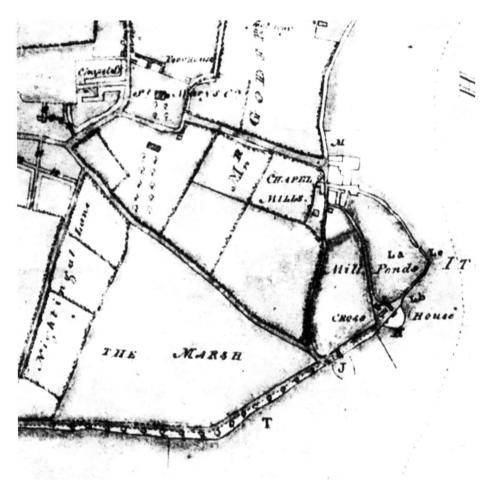

*A map of 1800 shows the Chapel area of Southampton as mainly agricultural or marsh lands and timber mill ponds stretching southwards to the sea, where there was a quiet shoreline before the docks were built. The future streets of houses would densely pack this area.*

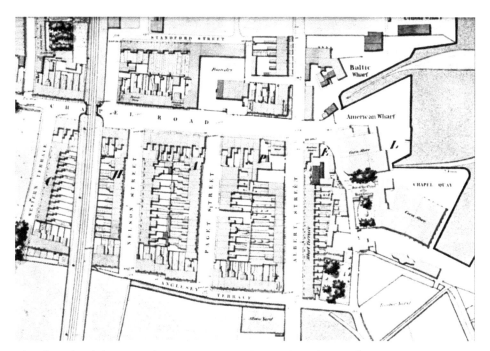

*Chapel Road and the surrounding streets in 1846 showing the early rows of terraces and the riverside wharves. The site of the original Trinity Chapel is just south of the corn store at the American Wharf. Bottom right are the yards and timber ponds of Crosshouse, while the London to Southampton Railway runs down the left (Crown Copyright).*

Terrace and Dock Street appeared around this period. Many of the old timber ponds at Crosshouse had been filled in and sold off by 1872, as the need for more building land became acute. Wharf Street was in evidence in 1884, Deal Street in 1887 and River Street (Endle Street) in 1897.

At Crosshouse, Southampton Corporation extended the Chapel Wharf, incorporating a refuse incinerator in 1885, a by-product of this being steam to pump the local sewage system. The remaining timber ponds, mills and associated businesses remained active until World War Two.

Tragedies tend to unite people, and the locals had their fair share over the years. Having been through the horrors of the Titanic disaster, the Great War and several periods of depression, the Chapel community was once again ravaged by the wartime Blitz in 1940/1 when many homes and lives were lost. Sitting between the Docks, the Supermarine Works and the Thornycroft shipyard at Woolston, Chapel's location had been the nature of its

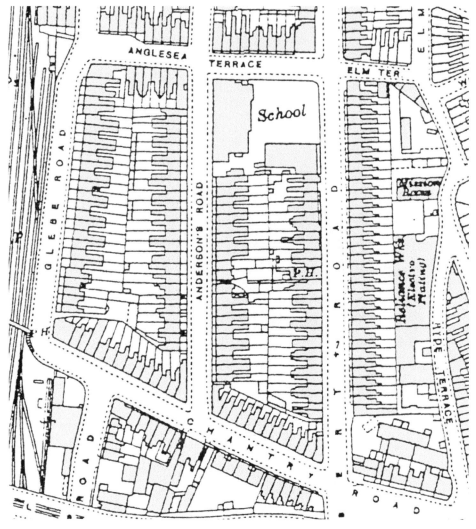

*The continued development south of Anglesea Terrace saw the arrival of Anderson's, Glebe and Chantry Roads. This map from 1933 shows the area before the Blitz (Crown Copyright).*

success, but now that became a curse. Enemy bombs rained down in a bid to obliterate those industries and the streets of Chapel were in the middle of it all. Not that Chapel fared any worse than any of the other downtown neighbourhoods, they were all badly damaged, but it was a hammer blow from which it never really recovered.

Many of those that had moved away during the conflict never came back, while others found they had nowhere to come back to. The post-war austerity years did little to help it

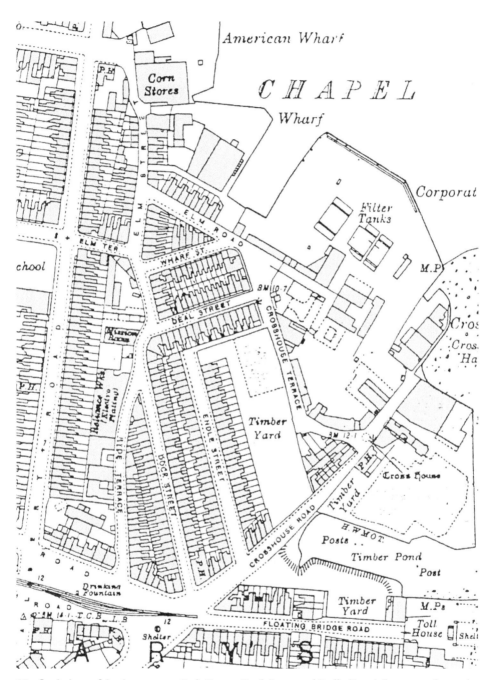

*The final phase of development saw Ryde Terrace, Dock Street and Endle (River) Street, together with Elm Road, Wharf and Deal Streets, built on the reclaimed timber ponds. Until the late 1950s it was still possible to walk directly from Chapel Road to Crosshouse via Elm Road and Crosshouse Terrace (Crown Copyright).*

*Looking north up Albert Road in 1968, after the bulldozers had done their work. In the left foreground is the corner of Chantry Road, while on the right are the remains of Tagart's Sawmill. On the extreme right can be seen the Ryde Terrace Foundry. Immediately ahead in the distance is the gasworks and the American Wharf is to the right. The tall building on the left is the former Eastern District School, which still stands after conversion to apartments within the new development (Dave Marden).*

back on its feet but, as ever, the people of Chapel got on with life as best they could. The gaps in the houses, where the wartime rubble had been cleared away, were rarely filled and were left as weed-covered open spaces that remained until the end finally came in the mid-1960s. In the preceding years, the council had already removed many homes in slum clearance and rehousing programmes. There was little left of Wharf Street, Deal Street or Ryde Terrace by the end of the 1950s, although Endle Street had some resurgence with a few light industries being relocated there; but now, the remaining streets of battered houses were showing severe signs of decay. Many were crumbling structures, having been built a hundred or more years before. They were systematically pulled down and by 1967, Chapel had virtually vanished altogether, with just the odd building left standing.

After clearance, the area became something of a wilderness of lorry parks and temporary buildings along with a few industrial depots, and the only real change came with the construction of the Itchen Bridge in 1974, which overlooked the whole sorry expanse. But after so many decades of desolation the streets breathed life again, this time with the redevelopment of the old Marsh area which, from 2003, saw the resurrection of the land between Chapel Road and Chantry Road. The smart, new apartments are a far cry from the homes that went before them – but I doubt they will last a hundred years like their predecessors!

Tracing the evolution of a street and its occupants over many generations can be a difficult task, as buildings change their identities over time. Buildings, sometimes, whole streets, become renumbered, while some corner properties can even change identities by moving into an adjacent street!

Residents came and went, often moving from street to street, or sometimes occupying several addresses in the same street. As many of these were seafarers they probably were not tied to a specific address, taking lodgings wherever available between voyages. The older directories list the trades and professions of residents and, apart from the usual smattering of mariners, engineers, boiler makers and shipwrights, there is the occasional vague reference such as 'of the docks'.

I have shown the streets in their entirety as they were prior to World War Two and indicated street numbers as they were at the time of their demise. This may differ to how they appeared at various stages in the past, but it is how most people would remember them. Other buildings that had previously disappeared are also displayed and referred to in the text.

# CHAPTER 2.

## Chapel Road

W here better to begin our visit than Chapel Road, as it is the oldest in the neighbourhood, having been an ancient thoroughfare and well established in mediaeval times. Originally conveying travellers from the lower town to the Trinity Chapel down by the River Itchen, it is by far the most interesting of the Chapel streets, mainly due its variety of buildings that included a large mixture of shops and businesses in amongst the residences. Unlike many of the surrounding streets that were laid down complete from the outset, the groups of buildings here evolved piecemeal.

In the 1811 street directory only a handful of residents were listed in the vicinity of Chapel Road, or Chapel Lane as it was previously known, those being mainly centred around the warehouses at Chapel Quay; but by 1836, the local population had swollen to around three dozen, including a grocer, watchmaker, dressmakers and a couple of tailors, plus, of course the inevitable beer retailers! Among the established residents were shipwrights and master mariners and, by that time, the Chapel Iron Foundry was well established under the ownership of Joseph West. By 1843, the street had developed further and, at this time, by using a latter-day plan as a key, we can locate the following premises.

## CHAPEL ROAD –
## NORTH SIDE, NOS. 1–19

One of the early residences would appear to be a large house adjacent to St Mary's Church. This was home to Benjamin Ransom, and later his son William, who were market gardeners, but Nos. 1–4, then named Chapel Terrace, were later erected on the site between the churchyard and Short Street (previously known as Church Street) in the mid-1800s.

No. 1 Chapel Terrace was originally a greengrocer's before becoming a haulage contractor's premises for much of the early 20th century, until the end of World War Two. It then became home to an electrical distribution firm. The other three were residences that housed a variety people such as gas fitters, a clerk and an 'entertainer' over the years.

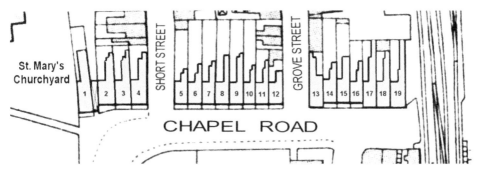

*The north side of Chapel Road between St Mary's Church and the railway crossing had interesting beginnings.*

The next row of buildings between Short Street and Grove Street was known as Elliot Place, having been erected in the 1830s. Nos. 5–11 were all residences but No. 12 was originally a beer retailer run by the Soles family, then a grocer's shop, before becoming the premises of bootmaker William Stockwell in 1849.

*Nos. 1–4 Chapel Road between St Mary's Church on the left and the corner of Short Street (Southampton City Archive).*

*Chapel Road showing Nos. 5–8 from the corner of Short Street (Southampton City Archive).*

*Chapel Road buildings Nos. 9–12 at the corner of Grove Street (Southampton City Archive).*

*Looking west along Chapel Road from the entrance to Grove Street. The Apollo Inn is on the right of the photo, taken about 1915 (Dave Marden Collection).*

Thirty-five-year-old George Gange ran the business in 1851, when the property was home to 12 people – the Gange family and three lodgers. Son William had taken over the business by 1876, and in 1881 was employing 7 men, 5 boys and 2 girls there, before opening premises on St Mary's Road and East Street. The shop was latterly occupied by the wholesale tobacconists of Riley & Davis.

No. 13 was the Apollo Inn, whose earliest proprietor, James Waters ran the establishment until 1850, when Francis Welsh took over. The pub carried on trading until closure in 1925 when it became a private residence and lasted until the final years of the street, along with its immediate neighbour. Nos. 14–16 were always private residences but the latter two became victims of wartime bombing – as did the remainder of this terrace.

No. 17 was first occupied by builder John Hill, until it became a fishmonger's throughout the latter half of the 19th century, after the builder had moved next door. Thus it remained until 1914, when it became yet another bootmaker's premises. No. 18 was a tailor's shop in its earliest days, and was occupied by builder John Hill (who had previously been at No. 17) until about 1860, and was subsequently a grocer's, stationer's and bootmaker's shop before reverting to greengrocery around 1912, staying as such until the 1930s.

*The corner of Chapel Road and Grove Street showing the former Apollo Inn at No. 13 (Southampton City Archive).*

No. 19 was the Railway Inn, which like its near neighbour, the Apollo Inn ceased trading in the 1920s. Its landlord was John Thursley, before it became a boot repair shop until reverting to a private residence a decade later. The land between No. 19 and the railway line was occupied by a number of coal merchants until the 1870s.

## CHAPEL ROAD – NORTH SIDE, NOS. 20–32 AND 33–42

On the eastern side of the railway tracks, starting from the corner of Standford Street, stood the Baltic Tavern (No. 20) belonging to Barlow's Victoria Brewery, taking its name from the nearby Baltic Wharf, and may previously have been known as The Stag. Its beer licence was established before 1869 but this was not surrendered until 1966 – long after the pub had been destroyed in the war.

No. 21 was at first a greengrocery shop until becoming a bakery run by William Evans from 1871, and latterly by Sarah Emily Evans until the 1920s, when it was badly damaged in a storm, after which it became a barber's shop. The buildings shown as Nos. 22 and

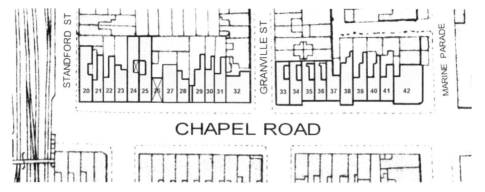

*The north side of Chapel Road that ran between the railway crossing and Marine Parade was a fine mixture of shops, pubs and businesses.*

23 were at one time known as Beach View and this would appear to have been a multi-tenanted building. The name is assumed because the buildings faced south across the then open marshland to the old town beach, that existed until construction of the docks began in 1838.

No. 24 was, in its early years, a lodging house run by a Mrs Elizabeth Draper (or Diaper) and No. 25 was (yet another) grocer's shop until the turn of the 20<sup>th</sup> century when Nos. 24 and 25 were jointly occupied by Prince & Sons the builders who traded there until at

*Chapel Road in 1915 was a busy main street with virtually everything to cater for the needs of the local population (Dave Marden Collection).*

*Sarah Evans' bakery shop at No. 21 Chapel Road, with severe damage in the aftermath of a storm (Dave Marden Collection).*

least 1975. No. 26 was at one time a hairdresser's, before joining the other ranks of grocery shops, while No. 27 belonged to a dairyman before it was taken over by the grocer's next door, and subsequently became operated by the Co-operative Society from around 1930.

The Co-op store lasted for over three decades before becoming the premises of a chemical preservation company. No. 28 had been a tailor's, a baker's and a pawnbroker's shop until reverting to a private residence in the 1930s.

No. 29 was the site of the Oriental Tavern in the 1840s, before becoming the General Dickson Arms from the 1850s until its closure in 1971. No. 30 was once a chemist shop and then a tobacconist before becoming a barber shop around 1920. Harry Bartlett ran the shop from the 1930s until its closure in 1971. Next door, No. 31 was yet another grocer's for most of its years until becoming West's Domestic Appliance shop in the 1950s. This business was one of the last survivors of the old street and the building still remains.

Harry Bartlett ran his barber shop in Chapel Road and cut my hair from the time I was a toddler until I was well into my twenties. He was a stocky, jovial sort with a bald head and a mad keen Saints fan, always closing early on match Saturdays to ride his bicycle to the Dell. The shop had two chairs, the one for kids was an old dentist's chair with a pedal that would raise the seat to what seemed halfway to the ceiling. If you were *really* small, he would place a plank of wood across the arms to raise you even higher.

At the entrance to the shop was a small counter, where Harry would sell such items as razor blades, combs and shaving soap, as well as other unmentionable things 'for the weekend'. In his spare time Harry was a special constable, the duties of which seemed to coincide with football at the Dell.

Getting your hair cut by Harry seemed to take an eternity. For a start, there was always a queue of people sat around the odd collection of chairs that lined the walls of the 'salon'. In the cold weather, one of these was always occupied by his one-bar electric fire that gave out so little heat you would have to sit on it to gain any benefit.

When it was eventually your turn in the chair he would ask what style you wanted – not that it mattered, as the end result was always short back and sides. Throughout the exercise there was only one topic of discussion – football! Harry would talk to all and sundry about last week's match or the one coming up. In between, he would be constantly interrupted by people coming into the front of the shop for various purchases, and my sessions in the chair always seemed to coincide with the arrival of one of his frequent cups of tea, brought in to him by Mrs West who ran the domestic appliance spares shop next door.

*The White Star on the corner of Chapel Road and Granville Street was a victim of wartime bombing, unlike the Arrow Inn opposite which survived (Dave Marden Collection).*

Eventually, when all was done, he would rub in a dollop of Brylcreem from a push-down dispenser that never seemed to run out. The final touch was the offer of a squirt of scent from a squeeze-bulb spray that was always accompanied with the words, 'Would you like a little of my hair restorer?'

Harry carried on cutting hair as long as he could, until his failing eyesight and trembling hands resulted in having your neck or ears nicked with increasing regularity, and he must have been well into his seventies when he finally decided to retire.

The final building in this section (No. 32), on the corner of Granville Street, began life as the Blue Anchor Inn, which was renamed the White Star around 1907 and belonged to Aldridge's Bedford Brewery. This pub dated back to the early 1860s, but closed in the

1930s when the building became a marine stores before becoming a victim of wartime bombing.

Granville Street was not constructed until around 1860, but to the east of its present site was the Chapel Iron Foundry run by Joseph West since the 1830s. When the foundry site was rebuilt in the 1840s, No. 33 was the Barge Tavern, standing on the corner of Chapel Road and Granville Street. It was renamed the Arrow Inn after the yacht *Arrow* which won the America's Cup in 1851 and was based in a nearby boatyard. Eldridge Pope were the owners of the pub, which finally closed on 23 October 1965.

No. 34 was, for most of its existence, a grocery shop before a brief conversion to a café after World War Two. It then became Mrs Zebedee's dyer and cleaner's shop for the remainder of its time. Nos. 35 and 36 were residences while No. 37 was a marine stores until World War One, and afterwards had a variety of uses until the 1960s.

No. 38 was originally the Princess Alexandra, owned by Welsh's Hyde Abbey Brewery until taken over by brewers Coopers. Its role as a pub ended around 1907 when it became a

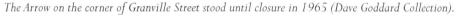

*The Arrow on the corner of Granville Street stood until closure in 1965 (Dave Goddard Collection).*

*The Durham Tavern stood on the corner of Chapel Road and Marine Parade. It was originally named the Floating Bridge Tavern (Dave Marden).*

cycle maker's shop, then after World War Two it belonged to a coal merchant before ending its days as a television repair shop. Next in line were four residences, Nos. 39–41.

In the late 1830s, No. 42 was the Floating Bridge Tavern on the corner of Marine Parade. This was later renamed the Durham Tavern around 1870 and belonged to Strongs of Romsey, before coming under the umbrella of Whitbread. There was previously a fifth house next door to the tavern, which at some time was absorbed by it when the licensed premises were extended. This pub was one of Chapel's last survivors, remaining until its licence lapsed on 21 October 1970.

# CHAPEL ROAD –
# SOUTH SIDE, NOS. 43–49, 50–58 AND 59–62

On the south side of the street, Loosemore's Hotel (No. 43) stood on the corner of Albert Road and was at one time known as the American Hotel, no doubt due to its proximity to the American Wharf. Its address was also recorded as No. 2 Albert Road. And the building appears to have been divided into two premises around 1850, with one half becoming a shop at No. 4 Albert Road. Before World War One a Telephone Calls Office was registered at the hotel (see *Albert Road*).

Moving westwards, there next follows a couple of shops and a residence. No. 44 was for many years a bootmaker's run by Charles Caws, until the 1920s saw it change to a greengrocer and general store before being destroyed in the Blitz. No. 45 was a residence briefly occupied by an umbrella maker in the 1880s, while No. 46 was a grocer's and a butcher's before becoming the long-established confectionery shop of the Galante family early in the 20th century, until the 1960s.

No. 47 was the home of a brush maker in 1884, but by 1907 it had become a fried fish shop which lasted until World War Two, after which it became a grocery shop until the final days under the name of Janmary, run by Arthur Lawes. No. 48 was for most of its time a greengrocer and fruiterers, but post-war became just a residence.

Janmary was always a very busy shop with tightly-packed shelves of jars, cartons and cans reaching high up to ceiling level. The cans on the top shelf were brought down with the aid of a long stick and expertly caught by Arthur Lawes in his other hand. Many of his

*Chapel Road's south side from Albert Road to the railway crossing, beginning with Loosemore's Hotel and including a great variety of shops.*

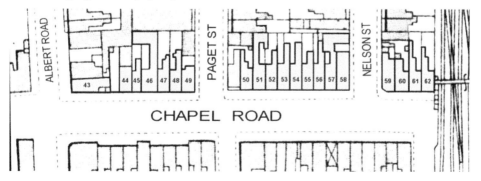

*The south side of Chapel Road showing Nos. 45–49 with the two shops of Galante and Janmary, with Kate's Bakery on the corner of Paget Street (Dave Marden Collection).*

customers bought their groceries 'on tick'. These were entered in a ledger and ticked off when payment was made at the end of the week.

At the end of this row, on the corner of Paget Street, No. 49 was a bakery. In fact, it was always such, right from the 1840s when Henry Emery was the baker. By the 1920s it was run by the Kerwood family, who had moved from nearby Melbourne Street. Charles Kates and Sons took over prior to World War Two until 1964 when, in its final days, it became Jarman's Cafe for a brief time until demolition.

Nos. 50–58 housed an assortment of trades. Back in the 1840s, No. 50 was the premises of Henry Ireland who was a bedstead maker, it then housed a variety of businesses before becoming Herbert's grocery store early in the 20th century and lasting until demolition in the 1960s.

No. 51 was, in the early days, a beer retailer's, from the mid-1800s until around the 1870s, when it was named Queen of the South and owned by Barlow's Victoria Brewery. It lost its licence in 1908 before becoming Edward Page's pork butcher's between the two world wars.

No. 52 was a bootmaker's shop belonging to Aaron Stevens from the mid-1800s. The Stevens family ran the business right up until World War One, after which it became a private residence. No. 53 was originally a tailor's shop run by John White in 1845, before becoming a fried fish shop in the early 1900s, remaining as such until it closed in 1966 under the ownership of Saltana Romano and his wife Doreen.

No. 54 was a butcher's shop from back in 1843, when it was run by Richard Stroud, and came under several ownerships until the firm of Eastman's took over in the early 1900s and ran it until the mid-1950s. No. 55 was always a private residence as was No. 56, until it became a hairdresser's under several ownerships until Thomas Roach was the last of the line in 1966.

Roach was a tall man and 'Lofty's Barbers' was quite a spartan place with an armchair in an almost empty room, and no electricity apart from that which supplied a very dim light bulb over the chair. Lofty had no set hours and could always be called to cut your hair at any time by a knock on his door, but this could often be a painful experience as his manual clippers seemed to pull out more hair than they cut.

*A wide variety of businesses occupied the buildings of Nos. 50–58 Chapel Road between Paget Street and Nelson Street (Dave Marden Collection).*

No. 57 was for many decades a greengrocer's shop run by the Finn family, from the early 1900s until the business ended with E. Davis in the 1950s. No. 58, on the corner of Nelson Street, was another butcher's shop from the 1840s, under several owners until Ernest Chard took over the business in the 1920s and ran it until closure around 1965.

From Nelson Street to the railway crossing were four premises. No. 59 was originally a beer retailer's run by Charles Scorey in the 1840s, before it became a grocer's shop in the 1860s. It then became variety of businesses until settling as dining rooms between the two world wars. Ronaldo Spagagna established his boot repair shop at that address after World War Two, until it closed in 1966.

No. 60 was originally named Chapel House and was, in the 1840s, a grocery store before it became a post office for a short while. By 1914 it was Martin & Co.'s confectionary shop, and then a newsagent's in the 1930s, before becoming a ladies' hairdresser's and finally a betting shop run by Painters until around 1970.

Across the railway line level crossing were three buildings (63–65) known as Enfield Place. The first of these was removed when the railway was widened and a signal box erected on the site. No. 65 (sometimes listed as No. 1 Western Terrace), stood on the corner of

*Chapel Road at the junction of Nelson Street approaching the railway crossing on the far right (Dave Marden Collection).*

Western Terrace and was another grocery shop in its early days prior to being a furniture dealer's around 1900, before becoming victim to wartime bombs.

The remainder of Chapel Road's south side from Western Terrace to St Mary Street was the grounds and residence of the Chantry, home to the clergy of the church opposite, together with St Mary's School for junior girls and infants.

# CHAPTER 3.

## Streets North of Chapel Road

As businesses and industries began to grow, several streets ran off the main thoroughfare of Chapel Road. On the north side were Short Street, Grove Street, Standford Street and Granville Street, leading to Melbourne Street, Marine Street, Princess Street, West Place and Longcroft Street. Of these, I have not included Grove Street, as much of it was within the St Mary's area (a subject this author may revisit in the future). I have devoted a separate chapter to Melbourne Street as this was quite a substantial thoroughfare.

### SHORT STREET

Short Street, as its name suggests, wasn't that long! It was a cul-de-sac tucked under the shadow of the old Workhouse (now the City College). It was initially named Church Street with just 21 houses. The site was a former orchard between Grove Street and St Mary's Church.

On the west side, No. 1A was a very small house, originally named Church Cottage, that looks to have been no more than two rooms – one above the other. One of its longest

*The houses in Short Street, showing the tiny No. 1A to Princess Cottages on the west side.*

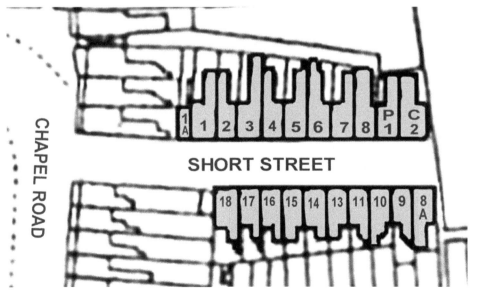

*No. 1A Short Street, seen on the left of the picture, must have been one of the smallest houses in Southampton (Southampton City Archive).*

*Nos. 4–8 on the west side of Short Street (Southampton City Archive).*

*The two Princess Cottages are on the right of the photo, at the end of Short Street's west side (Southampton City Archive).*

*Nos 8A to 10 on the east side of Short Street with No 8A on the left, next to the alleyway that led to Golden Grove and Grove Street*

*Nos. 11–15 on the east side of Short Street (Southampton City Archive).*

*The east side of Short Street with Nos. 15–18 (Southampton City Archive).*

residents was the Manly family, who were there from World War One until the late 1930s. The last two homes on that side of the street were Nos. 1 and 2 Princess Cottages. The numbering continued on the east side of the street with No. 8A and ran to No. 18 back towards Chapel Road. Oddly, there was no No. 12. At the northern end of the street, an alleyway led off to Golden Grove and Grove Street.

## STANDFORD STREET

Leaving Chapel Road just to the east of the railway crossing was Standford Street. The early street directories show this as Stamford Street, dating from the 1840s and running east–west parallel to Chapel Road, which it joined by way of a short north–south section alongside the railway level crossing.

## STANDFORD STREET –
## NORTH SIDE NOS. 1–16

The initial houses in Standford Street were on the south side, Nos. 1–12, but, when the northern side of the street was built, these all changed with Nos. 1–5 being a short terrace at the western end between the railway and Melbourne Street. Nos. 6–16 continued eastwards to

*The north side of Standford Street after renumbering. The buildings on the corners of Melbourne Street were both public houses, that were once numbered 5 and 6. No. 4 became part of the Bell and Crown pub.*

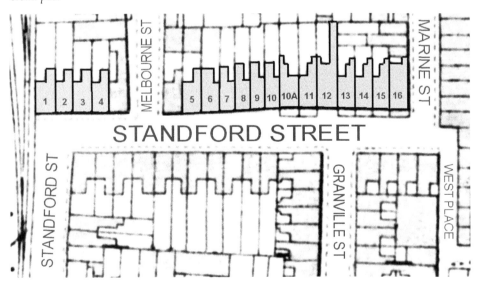

Marine Street, then resumed on the south side of the street with 17–19 as far as Granville Street, with 20–30 heading back to the railway. Nos. 31 and 32 were separate from the main street and appeared later on the short stretch that led to Chapel Road. In the 1880s the various trades of the residents included gas stoker, fireman, carman, midwife and needlewoman, together with the usual mariners and labourers.

The short terrace of Nos. 1–5 was reduced when No. 5 became No. 40 Melbourne Street. This building was initially the British Queen pub run by Thomas Bell, who also had stables there for his carriage business. It later became the Bell & Crown and subsequently absorbed No. 4 from Standford Street. After initially belonging to Cooper's Brewery, it was later taken over by Watney and was subject to a compulsory purchase by the local council in 1966, before its eventual demolition.

A pub on the opposite corner of Standford Street, the South Western Arms, run by F. Marshall, became No. 39 Melbourne Street. Owned by Aldridge's Bedford Brewery, William Green was the landlord in the 1870s, then several others held the licence before it closed in 1906. Afterwards, it became a private residence until being destroyed in the wartime bombing.

No. 12 was the Rifleman's Arms belonging to Barlow's Victoria Brewery, where George Bennett was in charge during the 1870s. Like its near neighbour, the South Western Arms, it closed in 1906 and became a general store under a succession of proprietors until it disappeared following wartime bombing.

No. 16 was another pub, named the Three Crowns, which belonged to the Old Shirley Brewery. It had a succession of proprietors and was taken over by Crowley's Alton Brewery before it closed in 1907, with Thomas Budd in charge. It then had several private residents before becoming yet another victim of wartime bombs. In fact, the complete terrace from 5–16 was lost, leaving only Nos. 1–3 intact.

## STANDFORD STREET – SOUTH SIDE NOS. 17–30 AND NOS. 31 AND 32

On the south side of Standford Street, Nos. 20–24 were also destroyed in the war. These housed several long-term families with the Wareham's living at No. 22 and the Hatch's at No. 23, both resident from pre-World War One days until the Blitz. In the 1880s, No. 27

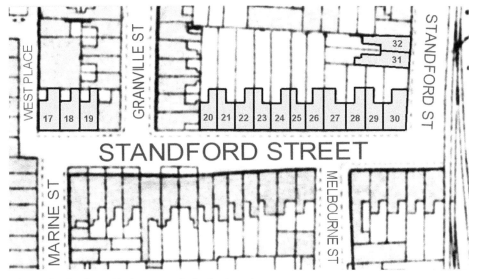

*The south side of Standford Street with the final numbering system which included Nos. 31 and 32, the two houses on the section leading to Chapel Road. These lasted until the 1920s.*

*Residents pick their way through the remains of Standford Street in September 1940. Looking east towards Marine Street and West Place, with Granville Street on the right. The taller houses in the distance are in Marine Parade (Southampton City Archive).*

*Nos. 1–3 and No. 30 at the western end of Standford Street can be seen in this photo behind the locomotive. The Bell and Crown pub sign is just visible through the steam. The large building to the right is the engineering works of Prince & Son (Dave Marden Collection).*

was a bootmaker's, but became a general shop around the turn of the century and seems to have closed as a business at the outbreak of World War Two. Miss A. Clark took over the tenancy of No. 30 from her mother around 1914 and remained in residence until the mid-1950s. Another long-standing tenant was William Hooker, who lived at No. 28 from the end of the war until the building was demolished in the 1960s.

## GRANVILLE STREET

The next street branching off from the north side of Chapel Road was Granville Street, again, a very short terrace leading to Standford Street. This was built a couple of decades after some of its Chapel counterparts, appearing around 1860, linking Chapel Road with Standford Street across the site of the former Iron Foundry of Joseph West. As with others of the time, its numbering system changed around 1870 as more streets grew around it. By the 1880s the residents consisted of boat builders, ship's firemen, carpenters and a laundress. At that time, No. 15 was a general shop run by Benjamin Pounds.

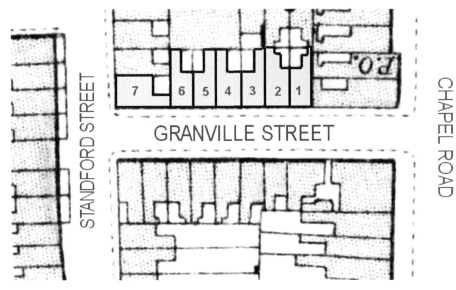

*The east side of Granville Street showing Nos. 1–7 in 1910.*

Nos. 6–9 were lost to wartime bombing but the rest of the street survived until demolition. Walter Hurst had lived at No. 5 since before World War One until the street was pulled down around 1964.

*Granville Street's west side showing house Nos. 8–15*

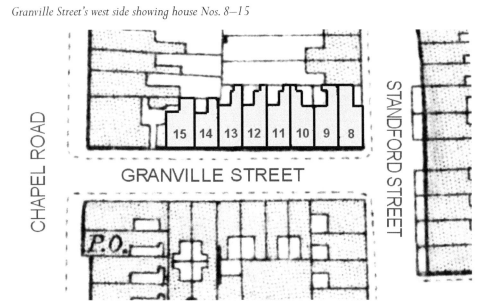

*Above and below showing Nos. 7 and 8 Granville Street, that were early victims of wartime bombing. Both photos were taken from Standford Street, which was itself badly damaged by air raids (both Southampton City Archive).*

## PRINCESS STREET

Not to be confused with Princes Street that lies further north at Northam, Princess Street ran between Melbourne Street and Marine Parade. On the north side of the street were Nos. 1–10 with a yard taking up much of the area towards Marine Parade. No. 1 was originally the building on the corner which was a baker and grocery shop, and later renumbered as 38 Melbourne Street. Frederick Gange appeared in the 1907 directory as living at No. 2 until the 1930s, while another long-serving resident was Henry Rogers at No. 1 from 1914 until the Blitz, after which only No. 3 remained in occupation until the street disappeared under the gasworks expansion of the 1960s.

No. 11 was on the south side, on the corner of Marine Street, and the numbers continued west towards Melbourne Street. These buildings had more variety than their neighbours opposite. No. 12, on the corner of Marine Street, was a public house and is shown on the 1816 map as the Engineers Arms, but later was known as The Wonder before becoming the Foresters Arms from the 1880s until its closure in 1924, after which it remained as a residence until its destruction by bombing in 1940. The numbering system on the south side was, at one time, haphazard with five dwellings being cottages with names back in the

*The north terrace of Princess Street showing Nos. 1–10. To the right of the houses was a onetime coal yard and the building at the end of the street was Marine Lodge which fronted onto Marine Parade.*

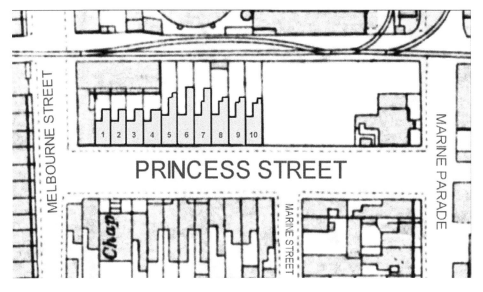

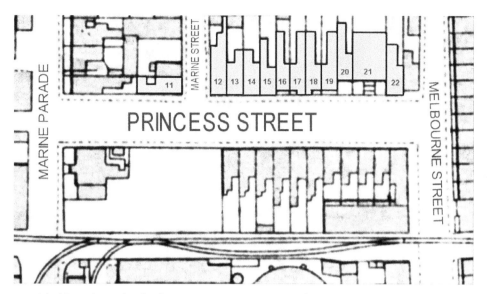

*Nos. 11–22 on the south side of Princess Street were a variety of buildings, with No. 12 as a public house and several cottages at Nos. 15–19, with a chapel at No. 21. No. 22 was a general shop until it went out of business in the 1930s.*

1860s. These were Sussex Cottage (latterly No. 15), Cyprus Cottage (No. 16), Laburnum Cottage (No. 17), Myrtle Cottage (No. 18) and Rose Cottage (No. 19).

No. 20 was the residence of the mission keeper who looked after the chapel at No. 21. This was originally the Bible Christian Chapel in the 1870s and in the next decade it became St Mary's Mission Chapel, a 'Working Men's Club and Reading Room'. By 1912 it had been renamed the Chapel of the Good Shepherd, but during World War One it was a mere store for Drinkworth's Potato Merchants. By the 1930s it was used by S. Chadwick, who were steamship furnishers. After that, the building appears to have been a residence before succumbing to wartime bombing. Since the early 20th century No. 22 was a general shop, which seems to have gone out of business in the 1930s before becoming yet another victim of the bombing. Only Nos. 17–20 remained in place after the war until the street was engulfed by the growing gasworks in the 1960s.

## MARINE STREET

Marine Street was a short terrace at the end of Standford Street, tucked behind Marine Parade. Seven houses and a yard formed the east side while, on the opposite side, a couple

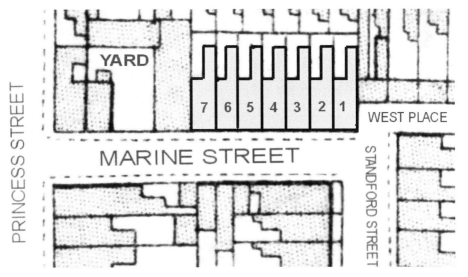

*The small terrace of seven houses along the east side of Marine Street between West Place and Princess Street. Further along was a yard, initially a blacksmith's, which finally belonged to a coal merchant.*

of dwellings were tucked between the properties of Princess Street and Standford Street. Residents' names first appeared in the street directory of 1863, when the usual mariners, shipwrights, bootmakers, labourers and a cook made up the population. The yard was evident from the 1880s when it was a wheelwright and blacksmith's shop run by the

*The west side of Marine Street had only two houses (Nos. 8 and 9) listed until No. 10 appeared in the 1930s. Its precise location is uncertain.*

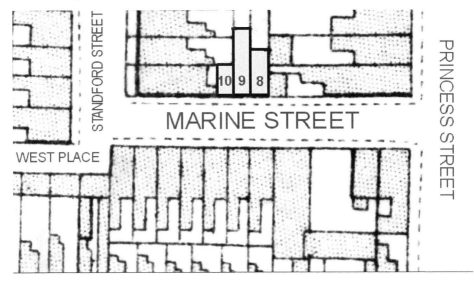

Trimmer family until the mid-1920s, when Ernest Trimmer diversified into building motor bodies. In the 1930s cartage contractor Frank Bundy briefly took over the yard, which seems to have fallen out of use until taken over by coal and coke merchant J. Adams in the 1950s. By the mid-1960s Marine Street, along with Princess Street and Standford Street, had been taken over by an extension of the gas company's works.

## WEST PLACE

West Place was a tiny street in two parts that ran at right angles to each other. The first section ran east–west from Marine Parade and Nos. 1 and 2 were on the south side. The second section ran north–south and had three houses, Nos. 3, 4 and 5. In early days there

*The dog leg street that was West Place, showing Nos. 1–5 and the site of the original farrier's yard.*

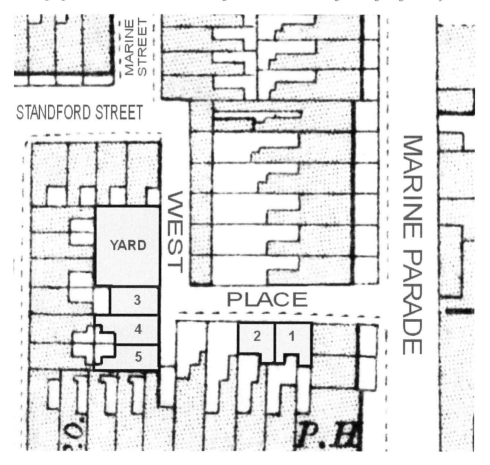

*Looking south along Nos. 3–5 West Place. The taller buildings at the back are in Chapel Road (Southampton City Archive).*

was also a yard which served as a farrier, smithy and wheelwright's shop run by John Sharp in the 1870s and 1880s. This seems to have disappeared when the site was cleared around 1900.

No. 1 was originally a lodging house and in 1871 it was run by a Mrs Hallett. In later years it had become a greengrocer's shop, where the proprietor was a Mr Frank Snook in 1871. Nos. 1 and 2 disappeared in World War Two as a result of bombing.

The three houses along the other section were originally numbered 1–3 but became Nos. 3–5 around 1870. The Sherin family lived at No. 4 from 1907 until the 1950s, and this was the last one occupied in 1967.

# CHAPTER 4.

## *Melbourne Street*

L eading off Standford Street, Melbourne Street was another of the earlier streets in the Chapel area with houses shown on the 1846 map as several groups with different numbering systems – or no numbers at all. It ran north–south from Bevois Street down to Standford Street, to the west of the town's gasworks, which at that time was quite a small facility but later grew to engulf much of the area.

About a third of the way down, the street was crossed by a public footpath. On the east side was the original entrance to the gasworks, appropriately named the Gas Cut, which was part of the Golden Grove Footway that connected to Marine Parade. It continued on the west side of the street as an alleyway between Nos. 72 and 73, leading to a footbridge over the main railway line where the alley continued to Grove Street and Golden Grove.

## MELBOURNE STREET –
## EAST SIDE NOS. 1–16

The east side of the street was numbered 1–16 from Bevois Street southwards to the Gas Cut, and then 17–36 at the tramway crossing. Nos. 37–39 were south of the crossing before reaching Standford Street. On the east side, the numbers ran 40–52 from Standford Street below the tramway crossing, then 53–72 at the Gas Cut, and finally 73–88 back to Bevois Street. There was, at one time, a number 89 which appeared in the 1863 directory, but this probably became part of the adjoining Queen's Head public house that stood on the corner of Bevois Street.

No. 1 Melbourne Street was home to gas inspector William Smith in the 1880s and, before World War One, it was the abode of cartage contractor R. Kelsey. No. 11 was at one time a shop run by Mrs Lydia Martin, from the 1880s until 1912.

As was befitting in this area, with its thirsty gas workers and those from the nearby wharves, there were a number of pubs in the street, two of which stood astride the entrance to the gasworks itself.

*Looking north-east to Nos. 13–16 Melbourne Street in the aftermath of wartime bombing. Nearest the camera is No. 16, formerly the Ganneymeade Inn, which closed in 1927 (Southampton City Archive).*

*Nos. 1–16 on the eastern side of Melbourne Street. The cut way by No. 16 was once part of the Golden Grove footway which continued across the street and over a footbridge to Grove Street.*

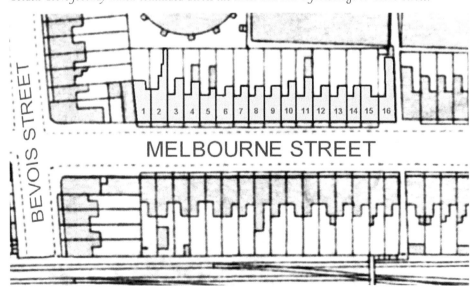

No. 16 was the Ganneymeade Inn, on the corner of the Gas Cut works entrance. It was originally named The Fox and was No.1 before the street was renumbered in the opposite direction. George Cobb was one of the early landlords in the 1850s under the old name, but Alfred White was the final licensee when the pub closed in 1927. After becoming a private residence, Henry Diaper was its last tenant when the building, along with its neighbours from 7–15, suffered wartime bombing.

## MELBOURNE STREET – EAST SIDE NOS. 17–36

On the southern side of the Gas Cut stood another pub. This was the John Barleycorn at No. 17, owned by the Winchester Brewery. In 1863 it was run by Richard Applin, who was listed as a carpenter and beer retailer. The name 'Barleycorn' first appeared in the 1880s when Thomas Blake was in charge. Like many nearby pubs, it lost its license in 1908 when Albert Wareham was its final landlord.

Nos. 7–16 were victims of wartime bombs which accounted for many homes in the area, while Nos. 1–6 survived until around 1960 when the gasworks expanded and took over that side of the street.

No. 25 had always been a shop, from the time James McCarthy ran it in the 1850s until the 1880s, after which it was briefly a beer house but reverted to a shop at the turn of the century. The Bundy family ran the business from 1912 until it was destroyed in the war. Nos. 26–30 appear to have been removed around 1898 when the gas company's works expanded and took over the Gas Cut, Godfrey Street and part of Longcroft Street.

Wartime bombing accounted for Nos. 17–33, and the remaining Nos. 34 and 35 survived but were also removed when the gasworks expanded around 1960.

No. 35 was the Melbourne Arms where, back in 1871, John Holly was listed as coal meter and beer retailer. The pub was owned by Scrace's Star Brewery from 1892, but was later taken over by Strongs of Romsey before it closed in 1939. At that time the licensee was Mrs Louisa Tusler, who remained there as a private resident until the building disappeared around 1960.

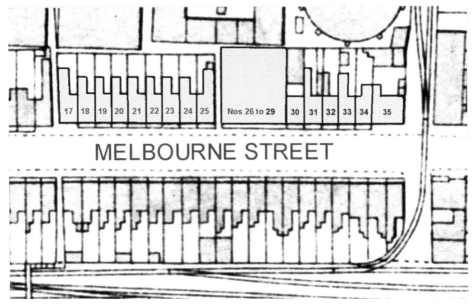

*The middle section of Melbourne Street's eastern side showing buildings Nos. 17–35 from the Gas Cut to the Chapel Tramway crossing. Nos. 26–29 did not appear in directories after the late 1800s.*

## MELBOURNE STREET –
## EAST SIDE NOS. 17–39

The final part of Melbourne Street's east side ran from the tramway crossing, past Princess Street and on to Standford Street. In the 1870s, No. 36 was the site of Hague's Steam Flour Mill, which seems to have ceased operation around 1880 but later became Pascoe's

*There were not many buildings on Melbourne Street's east side between the tramway crossing and Standford Street.*

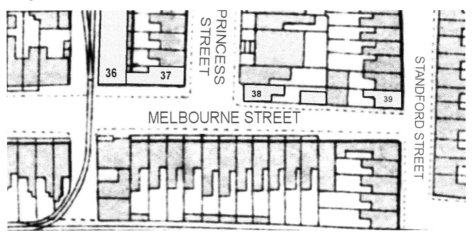

*The Co-op store at No. 37 on the corner of Melbourne Street and Princess Street. The tall building on the left is No. 36, the former steam flour mill (Dave Marden Collection).*

Upholsterers in the 1930s and, finally, Butler's Ship Stores at the end. By 1907, No. 37 had become a store run by the local Co-operative Society which lasted until the 1920s. No. 38, on the corner of Princess Street, was a grocery shop in the 1880s, then a bakery in the early 1900s. It was run by the Kerwood family from 1914 to around 1920, when they moved to nearby Chapel Road. It then became a grocer's once more, with Thomas Paglier running it until the outbreak of war. When hostilities ceased, Thomas was in residence there until the building came down in 1960. No. 39 was originally No. 6 Standford Street, where it was the South Western Arms (see Standford Street).

# MELBOURNE STREET –
# WEST SIDE NOS. 40–52

Returning northwards along the western side of the street from Standford Street to Bevois Street, this side of Melbourne Street became Nos. 40–88 under the later numbering system, with the Bell & Crown pub at No. 40. This was originally No. 5 Standford Street (see Standford Street). Next door, at what became No. 41, lived William Soper who was a shoemaker in the mid-1800s, and Nos. 41–51 were also all private residences.

The Bell & Crown pub was one of the last buildings to survive in Melbourne Street (Dave Goddard Collection).

South of the tramway at No. 52 stood the Mill Tavern (named after the mill opposite). It belonged to Edwards Botley Brewery and was run by Richard Cosens in its earliest days, then under the name of the Well Tavern. Henry Dear was licensee from the early 1900s until John Cole took over in the 1930s, being the final landlord when the building was destroyed

The bottom end of Melbourne Street's western side between No. 40 and 52, where the Bell & Crown at No. 40 was one of the last survivors when the area was cleared in the mid-1960s.

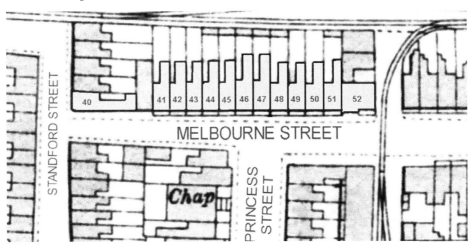

*A pre-World War Two photo of an engine on the Chapel Tramway, giving a glimpse of the Melbourne Arms on the right (Dave Marden Collection).*

in the war. At the same time, Nos. 41–47 were also lost in the bombing. However, Nos. 48–51 survived until the street was finally cleared in 1966.

# MELBOURNE STREET –
# WEST SIDE NOS. 53–72

The remaining residents on Melbourne Street's western side, Nos. 53–72 (and 73–88), fared better than their opposite neighbours in that most of their homes remained *in situ*

*The middle section of Melbourne Street's western side from the tramway to the Golden Grove footway with Nos. 53–72.*

until the 1966 clearance. Of these, only No. 62 seems to have fallen out of use before then, around 1960. In 1899, Nos. 53–56 had been purchased by the Chapel Tramway Company in order to realign the railway track that ran adjacent to them.

James Painter was a shopkeeper at No. 72, on the corner of the alleyway that led over the footbridge to Grove Street. He was there since the earliest days in the 1840s, until the 1880s – a tradition that was carried on until the shop closed around 1960. That was when all the buildings opposite had disappeared under the gasworks extension. Other long-serving proprietors were the Barton family from 1907–31 and, latterly, the Street family from 1939 until closure, with Mrs Street remaining in residence until the final days in 1966.

## MELBOURNE STREET – WEST SIDE NOS. 73–88

Another long-term business belonged to Alfred Terry who lived at No. 81, whose profession as a boot finisher flourished from 1907–31. George Broomfield lived at No. 88 from 1916–60, where he had spent the final 30 years as a chimney sweep. No. 83 was the only house in this group without a named occupant after 1960. All the others continued until the 1966 clearance.

*The final, northern section of Melbourne Street's western side, Nos. 73–88, continued until 1966. No. 89 appeared briefly in the 1863 directory and may have become an attachment to the Queens Head public house on the corner of Bevois Street.*

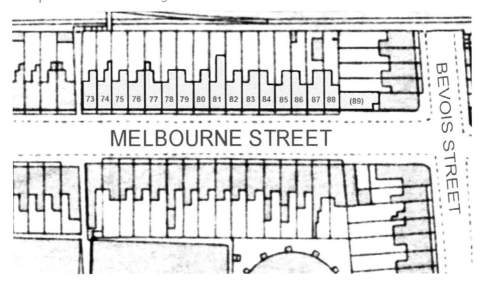

The railway from the wharves crossed Melbourne Street and joined sidings at the main line via a gate to the rear of No. 53. Westlake's sack factory stood on the far side of the main line in Grove Street (Bert Moody).

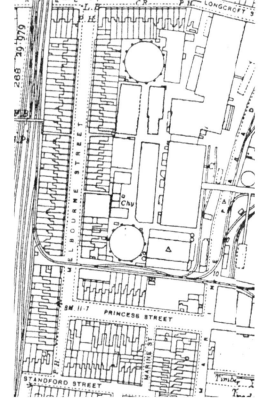

Melbourne Street in 1933.Within a couple of decades, the gasworks would expand and engulf the east side of the street, Princess Street and Marine Street. The railway to the wharves along Marine Parade is the Chapel Tramway which ceased operation in 1967 (Crown Copyright).

# CHAPTER 5.

## *Marine Parade and Godfrey's Town*

## MARINE PARADE

Marine Parade was another of the older streets in the Chapel area, running between Chapel Road and Belvidere Road, and alongside the wharves that lined the River Itchen. These, together with Chapel Wharf, were in operation long before the docks were built. Each of the wharves specialised in particular cargoes such as timber, slates and cement but the main commodity was coal, received in huge amounts from northern colliers, mostly to feed the insatiable appetite of the local gasworks. There were also several yacht and boat builders established there and many of these, together with their workforces, lived in the houses that lined the west side of the street.

Marine Parade also had its own industrial railway, the Chapel Tramway, which had a line running down the eastern side of the road, feeding sidings on the wharves. The railway turned west, just north of Princess Street, and crossed over Melbourne Street before joining the exchange sidings at the main line that ran down to the Terminus Station.

## MARINE PARADE –
## WEST SIDE NOS. 1–18

Most of the Marine Parade houses were grouped in two terraces between West Place and Princess Street, while others were towards the northern end of the street near Longcroft Street, an area once known as Godfrey's Town (see separate chapter on this) in the old settlement of Crabniton that sat between Chapel and Northam.

The 1846 map shows a row of houses numbered 1–6 which, in a later expansion of dwellings, became Nos. 3–8 in a line of 1–17 stretching from the Durham Tavern public house to Princess Street. Marine Lodge was a substantial building on the corner of Princess Street. In the old directories it is sometimes referred to as No. 18, but that number seems to have disappeared around the time of the gasworks expansion at the turn of the 20th century. However, the building remained in place, possibly for the works use, until the wartime bombs removed it.

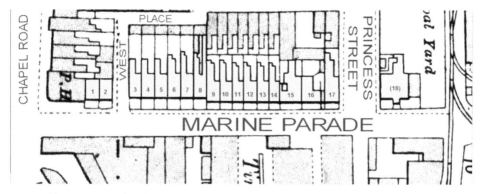

*Nos. 1–17 Marine Parade, where Nos. 3–8, as above, was the original terrace of three-storey houses numbered 1–6. The building shown as No. 18 was Marine Lodge, which appears to have been a multi-occupied building until that area was later swallowed up by the ever expanding gasworks.*

*Nos. 3–8 Marine Parade were numbered 1–6 when built, possibly in the 1830s, and were, at that time, considerably desirable properties (Dave Marden Collection).*

*No. 17 Marine Parade stood on the corner of Princess Street until destroyed in the war (Southampton City Archive).*

## MARINE PARADE – WEST SIDE NOS. 19–24

Still on the west side of Marine Parade, but further north towards Longcroft Street was another crop of buildings, formerly part of Godfrey's Town. This area was also swallowed up in the 1898 expansion of the gasworks. The original No. 18 was a timber merchant's belonging to George Sharp, back in the 1850s. In the next decade, the premises had been taken over by coal merchant James Bennett, who was still there at the turn of the century running a carting business. No. 19 belonged to another coal merchant, Ekless and Son, in the 1880s.

Back in the 1840s, No. 20 was the Britannia Hotel, run by a succession of landlords until it became a coffee house around 1884 under the ownership of Henry Cooke, but that venture did not last long as by the late 1880s it had become yet another coal merchant's. No. 21 belonged, at times, to a corn merchant, shopkeeper and coal merchant from the 1880s, until being enveloped by the gasworks. No. 22 belonged to coachman Joseph Golding back

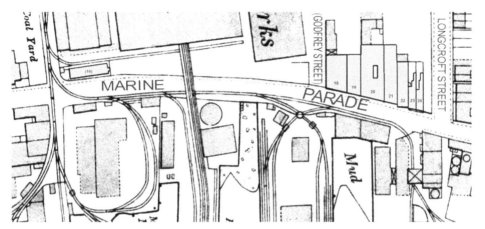

*On the above map, No. 19 was originally the Gas Company offices, but after being absorbed into the works (along with No. 18 Marine Lodge) those two numbers were applied to buildings further up the street. No. 20 was formerly the Britannia Hotel from the 1840s until the 1880s, when it became the Britannia Coffee Shop, but that venture didn't last long as it became a coal merchant's and then a store by the turn of the century, until the gas company extended its works over the site.*

in 1871, and yacht builder Dan Hatcher was the owner in 1876, but the boat building business had been taken over by Stephen Payne by the 1880s. No. 23 was a private residence from the 1870s, while No. 24 was a general store run by William Moreton.

At one time, from the 1850s, No. 24 was applied to the Mariner's Inn on the opposite corner of Longcroft Street. It belonged to Aldridge's Bedford Brewery with landlord Edmund Futcher at the helm, but Francis Fryer had taken over by the 1860s. By the 1880s its address had been changed to Belvidere Road, and the pub's ownership was Brickwoods at the time it ceased trading in 1934.

After the buildings around Godfrey's Town and Longcroft Street had disappeared in 1898, Nos. 18 and 19 were applied to Gas Company buildings in Marine Parade. The new No. 18 was given to Marine Lodge and No. 19 was taken by their offices. These were, in turn, eliminated by further developments in the gasworks.

# MARINE PARADE –
# WHARVES ON EAST SIDE

The east side of Marine Parade was lined with wharves along the River Itchen. These carried the names of places where the trade originally came from. They were once a collection

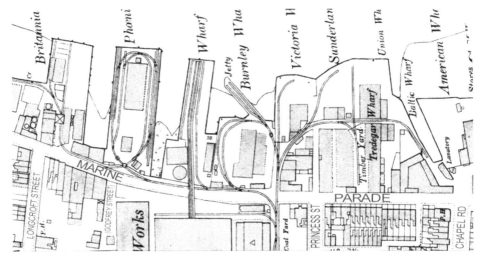

*The wharves along Marine Parade in 1910, showing the railway sidings linked by the tramway running along the street. Judging by the mud lines shown, it would seem that many of them were only accessible by vessels at high tide.*

of individually built wharves, but over time they have been greatly modified and joined together as a mainly uniform frontage. At one time, most were served by railway sidings linked to the main line by the Chapel Tramway, which ran along the main road. As trade from the wharves declined, only Britannia Wharf was using the railway, which finally ceased operation in 1967.

Baltic Wharf was given over to the corn and coal trade in the latter half of the 1800s, until the 1920s. Union Wharf was predominantly for the import of timber and a steam-operated sawmill operated until the turn of the 20th century, when the name was changed to Tredegar Wharf. Sunderland Wharf dealt mainly with the cement industry and Victoria Wharf handled coal, for many years operated by Edwin Jones & Co. Burnley Wharf was also handling coal where the firm of J. R. Wood was based until the 1920s, when they moved up river to Dibles Wharf at Northam. Phoenix Wharf also handled huge amounts of coal, mainly to feed the hungry retorts of the gas company's works. The coal was carried over Marine Parade and up to the retort houses by a system of conveyors that operated continuously day and night. Finally, Britannia Wharf was originally used for coal and cement, but from the 1870s until comparatively recent times it was occupied by builders' merchants, Hooper and Ashby.

An aerial view of Marine Parade taken in 1924, showing the wharves, the tramway and the sprawling gasworks in the foreground. Marine Lodge can be seen at the bottom right of the picture (Dave Marden Collection).

Looking north up Marine Parade towards the gasworks with a train on the Chapel Tramway (Bert Moody).

# GODFREY'S TOWN

Although not strictly in the Chapel area, Godfrey's Town was situated in the old neighbourhood of Crabniton which sat to the north of Chapel and was named after the landowner of that time. It has been included because of its relation to Marine Parade and the gasworks.

In 1800, Mr Godfrey's estate covered the area from what is now Northam Road down as far as Marsh Lane. A small village grew up, bounded by Longcroft Street, Marine Parade and, appropriately, Godfrey Street. The fourth boundary was an alleyway called Godfrey's Passage that ran between the western ends of Godfrey Street and Longcroft Street.

Godfrey's Town on the 1846 map shows 15 buildings along Godfrey Street, including the Victory public house which was No. 1. It was owned by Barlow's Victoria Brewery and its early landlord was John Powell. The Biffin family were licensees from the 1860s until the late 1880s, after which its name had changed to the Godfrey Inn by the time it closed around the turn of the century.

*The 1846 map of Godfrey's Town, showing Godfrey Street and the Victory public house, which was No. 1 (Crown Copyright).*

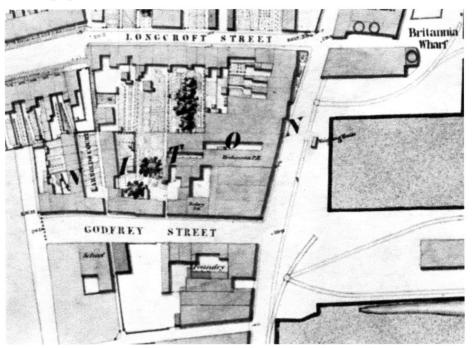

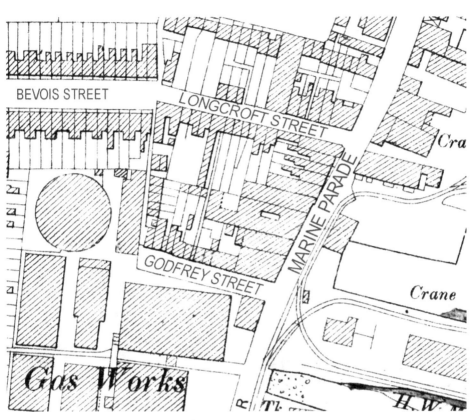

BEVOIS STREET

LONGCROFT STREET

GODFREY STREET

MARINE PARADE

Cra

Crane

Gas Works

H.W.

*Godfrey's Town in 1897, where many of the buildings between Longcroft Street and Godfrey Street were soon to be swallowed up by the imminent expansion of the gasworks (Crown Copyright).*

*A plan dated 1898 showing the areas of Godfrey's Town to be acquired by the gas company, which already had a considerable presence. The building shown as the Godfrey Inn was formerly the Victory public house, and it would appear the numbers shown on the buildings are purely for the gas company records rather than street numbers (Dave Marden Collection).*

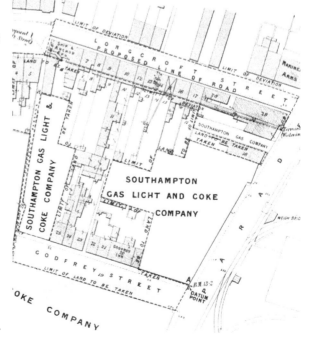

The numbers ran 1–9 westwards (to the left). The remaining six buildings were also numbered 1–6 in the opposite direction! To add to the confusion, the 1884 street directory also details Godfrey's Court (running from Longcroft Street to Marine Street) being numbered 1–14 and including many of the same residents' names.

Godfrey's Town all but disappeared when the gas company expanded its works at the turn of the 20th century and took over most of the land between Longcroft Street and Princess Street, leaving just a few buildings fronting Marine Parade, until they too were built on in the early 1900s.

## LONGCROFT STREET

Longcroft Street, between Marine Parade and Bevois Street, was another of the early streets that appeared on the 1846 map and formed the northern boundary of Godfrey's Town.

*The Ship and Anchor was on the corner of Longcroft Street until it, and the entire street, was engulfed in the expansion of the gasworks (Dave Marden Collection).*

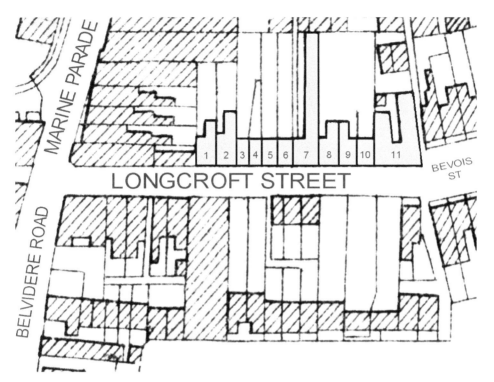

*The south side of Longcroft Street in 1897, with No. 11 as the Ship and Anchor pub. Soon, only the pub would remain, as the other buildings became victims of the gasworks expansion at the turn of the century.*

## LONGCROFT STREET –
## SOUTH SIDE NOS. 1–11

The south side was very straightforward, with a line of buildings running from east to west and numbered 1–11. No. 11 was the Ship and Anchor public house which existed from early Chapel days through to closure in August 1966. Ben Ransom was the licensee back in the 1840s when the pub belonged to Scrase's Star Brewery, but Strongs of Romsey had taken over early in the 20th century.

## LONGCROFT STREET –
## NORTH SIDE NOS. 12–32

The north side of Longcroft Street is something of a puzzle, because the houses were spread in a haphazard pattern and linked by yards and alleyways. Through a process of elimination,

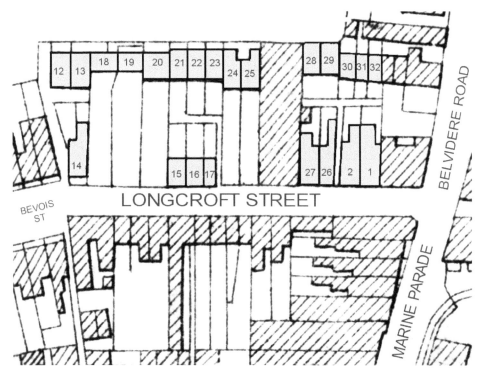

*Buildings to the north of Longcroft Street were scattered at intervals, with some laid well back from the roadway.*

it has been possible to identify Nos. 14, 24 and 25 as those last remaining after the gasworks expansion, but the others indicated are by way of an educated guess according to likely access.

In this maze of yards and alleyways numbering was probably in two groups, as 14–25 and 26–32. There were also two houses numbered as 1 and 2 *Longcroft Cottages*. These seem to have appeared in the 1880s. No. 1 was occupied by Mrs Fanny Murrey from the turn of the 20th century until the 1920s and was, at one time, listed as a shopkeeper. The shaded area between Nos. 25–28 was always an industrial premises, and at one time an ironworks.

The building next to cottage No. 1 on the corner of Longcroft Street and Belvidere Road is the Mariners Arms public house (see Marine Parade). With the exception of No. 14, those numbered 12–23 disappeared before World War One, but Nos. 14, 24 25, the Cottages, and Nos. 26–32 survived into the 1930s. Nos. 26–30 were gone by the early 1930s and, by 1939, all those to the north of the street had been cleared away.

# CHAPTER 6.

## *Albert Road*

I make no excuse for giving the utmost coverage to Albert Road. Firstly, it was probably the area's most prominent street after Chapel Road, being a very substantial thoroughfare and blessed with a large number of public houses – it was also my birthplace. Albert Road was another of the Chapel streets that developed piecemeal. It was originally laid down by the Floating Bridge Company in 1837 to connect the Itchen Wharves at Marine Parade with the Floating Bridge which had been opened a year earlier. The intention being to divert trade away from the Toll Bridge at Northam to the new ferry across to Woolston. It was initially known as Floating Bridge Road but, when the houses were built along it, that changed, with only the section near the Floating Bridge itself retaining the name.

We can look at the street in three sections. Firstly, from Elm Street to Elm Terrace; next, from Elm Terrace to Bridge Terrace (Chantry Road); and finally, Bridge Terrace to Royal Crescent Road at its southern end.

## ALBERT ROAD –
## EAST SIDE NOS. 1–39 (ALBERT TERRACE)

The first section, from Elm Street to what is now Elm Terrace, was called Albert Street and the houses on the eastern side were named Albert Terrace.

The Railway Tavern (No. 1) stood on the corner of Albert Street and Elm Street, having been built in the mid-1840s, and had Charles Robinson as landlord for two decades until the 1860s, with Christopher Childs and Albert Parsons each serving successive long stints either side of the turn of the century. The pub appears to have ceased trading in the 1920s and, after becoming a victim of wartime bombing, it stood in ruins for several years afterwards into the 1950s before it was finally cleared.

There is no record of No. 3, which was probably a yard with buildings between the Tavern and the beginning of Albert Terrace. All the dwellings were residences apart from No. 39 on the corner of Elm Terrace, which was a commercial premises, being that of a

*A late Victorian view of The Railway Tavern on the corner of Albert Road and Elm Street. The old corn warehouse on the American Wharf can be seen on the left background (Dave Marden Collection).*

*The remains of the Railway Tavern after its wartime bombing. It never reopened and the site was cleared in the 1950s (Dave Goddard Collection).*

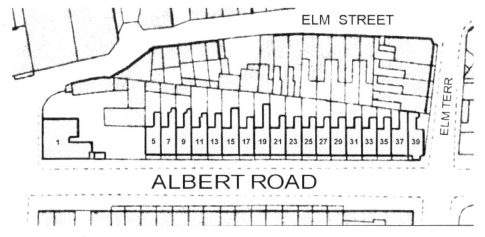

*The east side of Albert Road, showing what was Albert Terrace. No. 1 was the ill-fated Railway Tavern.*

beer retailer from the earliest days. Frederick and Mabel Chandler were hosts from 1920 until around 1950, when William Anderson ran it as a grocery shop which remained until the street was demolished in the 1960s. Nos. 25 and 29 were both, at some time, lodging houses. After these houses were demolished, the site became the City Refuse Yard.

*Nos. 5–11 Albert Road were part of the original Albert Terrace (Southampton City Archive).*

*Nos. 13–27 Albert Road, a continuation of the original of Albert Terrace (Southampton City Archive).*

*The southern end of the old Albert Terrace from Nos 27 to 39. No. 39 on the corner of Elm Terrace was originally a beer house, then a general store (Southampton City Archive).*

# ALBERT ROAD –
# WEST SIDE NOS. 2–40 (ALBERT STREET)

The west side of Albert Street (opposite Albert Terrace) ran from Chapel Road to Anglesea Terrace, where Nos. 2 and 4 were originally the American Hotel, so named because of its location near the American Wharf.

Master mariner Robert Loosemore, who was also a ship's chandler and brewer, occupied the premises from at least 1836 and applied his name to the hotel until the 1870s, when Charles Voller became the landlord. In the 1880s the building was divided in two, with the corner section being renumbered as 43 Chapel Road, retaining the name of Loosemore's Hotel, and the other half (No. 4) becoming a shop run by Thomas Simmons.

The hotel then had a succession of landlords (and landladies) and, by 1905, was in the hands of Frank Robinson and his wife and owned by the Gibbs Mew Brewery of Salisbury. A telephone calls office was incorporated there around 1912. Mrs Gertrude Fry took over during World War One and continued as its landlady until 1924, when its licence was withdrawn.

*The remains of Loosemore's Hotel on the corner of Chapel Road and Albert Road after wartime damage. By this time, it had been converted into two shops. The Durham Tavern can be seen on the far right of the picture (Dave Marden Collection).*

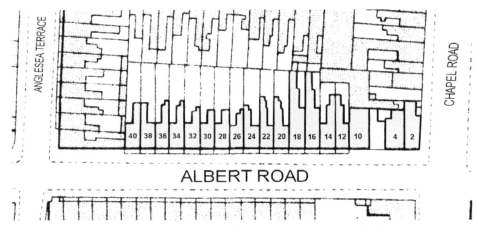

*The west side of Albert Street (later Albert Road) between Anglesea Terrace and Chapel Road.*

The building then became a pawnbroker's shop run by Abraham Cohen, and later by David Carr, while No. 4 continued as a general store run by the Batchelor family. Both premises were severely damaged in wartime bombing in 1940 and were then demolished.

There is no record of No. 6 but the site of No. 8 was the Albion Chapel Mission Hall until the turn of the 20th century. Furniture dealer William Jones then occupied the yard premises pre-World War One, with steel contractor Ellis Partridge and latterly corn merchant W. R. Holden taking over in the 1930s. This area of the street met the same fate as Nos. 2 and 4, and the site lay derelict until the remainder of the street was cleared away in the 1960s.

Nos. 10–18 were residences, and these also fell victim to wartime bombs. Stonemason Thomas Harris was one of the early occupants of No. 14, while, next door at No. 16, William Dark was a tea dealer and one-time accountant. Henry Stickland at No. 18 was a cattle dealer in 1884, being succeeded by two long-term tenants. Firstly, Harry West until the 1920s, before James Edwards moved in and lived there until the Blitz took its toll.

At No. 20, optician William Gamble was in residence in 1853, while the Dawson family had a long spell there for two decades from the mid-1930s. The Osman family were at No. 22 from at least 1912 until the mid-1930s. B. Royle was the final occupant of the whole terrace in 1970. Thomas Duffell (or Duffett) was a grocer at No. 28 in the 1840s–50s, while Thomas Sainsbury was an early beer retailer at No. 40 in 1843.

*Nos. 10–30, on the west side of Albert Road, were opposite Albert Terrace (Southampton City Archive).*

*Nos. 22–40 on the west side of Albert Road. No. 40 is on the left and was next door to the Anglesea Tavern (Southampton City Archive).*

# ALBERT ROAD –
# EAST SIDE NOS. 41–109 (RANSOM'S TERRACE)

Albert Road was extended southwards, from Elm Terrace to Bridge Terrace in 1842 with the east side named Ransom's Terrace, after John Ransom, a successful local man who had a shipyard at Crosshouse and owned the terrace where he housed many of his workers. On the corner of Elm Terrace stood a shop (No. 41) that was originally a grocer's from the 1860s, run by a Mrs Sarah Blewden until Emily Matthers took over in the early 1900s and also sold beer. At that time, Harry Curtis was living there and he had taken over by 1912, remaining in charge until the 1930s. The shop appears to have stopped selling beer prior to World War One and became a general store until its final days under Thomas Medley in 1966. No. 47 was the greengrocery business of F.& A. Curtis in the years prior to World War Two.

No. 109 was a grocery shop from the 1870s until the outbreak of that war, George Hurley being the proprietor for a couple of decades early in the 1900s. The property became a simple residence after World War Two, though an advert for Coleman's Mustard remained in place on the building until the end.

At the bottom of this section of the street was a sawmill, standing on the corner of Albert Road (Ransom's Terrace) and Bridge Terrace. It was initially operated by Charles Durdle from the early 1900s, until being taken over by Tagart, Morgan & Coles around

*Part of Ransom's Terrace on the east side of Albert Road, showing Nos. 41–81.*

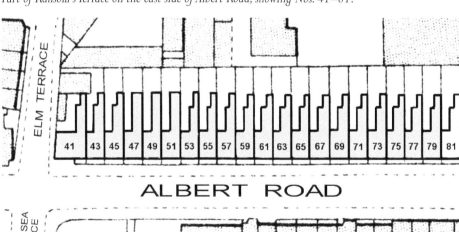

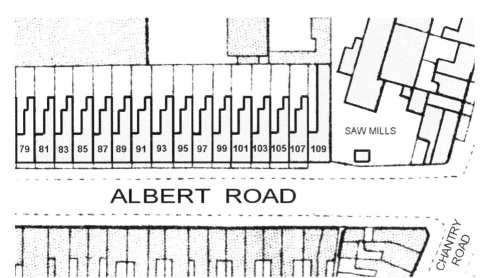

*The remainder of Ransom's Terrace at the bottom of Albert Road, showing Nos. 79–109 and the sawmills on the corner.*

*Part of Ransom's Terrace on the east side of Albert Road, showing Nos. 67–77 (Southampton City Archive).*

*More of Ransom's Terrace, which became Nos. 77–85 Albert Road (Southampton City Archive).*

*Another section of Ransom's Terrace, showing Nos. 83–93 Albert Road. Note the rare sight of a family car! (Southampton City Archive)*

*The final southern section of what was Ransom's Terrace, showing Nos. 95–109 Albert Road. No. 109 was originally a shop and the advertisement for Coleman's Mustard remained in place for many years after it became a residence (Southampton City Archive).*

1925, remaining so until closure in the 1960s. Tagart's was a great source of wood in off-cuts and there was always a mountain of shavings which were great for lining the floors of rabbit hutches – all this was given free!

# ALBERT ROAD –
# WEST SIDE NOS. 64–86 (ANDERSON'S TERRACE)

The section on the west side of Albert Road between Anglesea Terrace and Chantry Road was originally known as Anderson's Terrace (not to be confused with the neighbouring street Anderson's Road). On the corner of Anderson's Terrace and Anglesea Terrace was once the P&O Shipping Company's school, built privately to educate the children of their employees. This was eventually replaced by the Eastern District School around 1875 under the supervision of the town council, and later rebuilt in 1923 to the design that remains today. After World War Two it became the town's Technical College and in recent years it has been converted to apartments.

*The Three Swans pub stood at No. 84 Albert Road and was one of the last survivors of the street when it closed in 1967 (Dave Goddard Collection).*

No. 64 was firstly a grocer's shop when run by William Hales in 1884, and was briefly a baker's before becoming a general store once again around the turn of the century. It

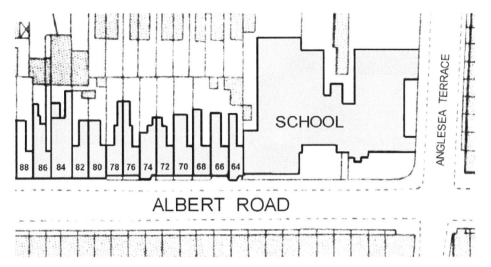

*Nos. 64–86 Albert Road – originally named Anderson's Terrace, and not to be confused with Anderson's Road which ran parallel to the west. The Eastern District School was a replacement for that previously provided by the P&O Shipping Company.*

was then a greengrocer's post-World War Two before its final phase as Dave Henton's motorcycle repair shop in the 1960s.

No. 80 was Sidney Doncom's hairdressers from the 1920s until about 1960. No. 82 was William Hurst's bootmaker's shop back in the 1880s for around twenty years, before it became a general store and then S. B. Lowman & Sons bakers prior to World War Two, ending its time as William Doran's greengrocer's in the 1960s.

No. 84 was the Three Swans, a pub that once had its own brewery and was leased to Eldridge Pope from 1866. Alfred Froud was the licensee from 1911 until the outbreak of World War Two. Then, apart from a brief spell of closure in 1941 due to wartime bomb damage, it continued serving pints until August 1967. My recollection of this pub was that you entered by a door on the right-hand side, into a gloomy passage with the bars leading off to the left.

The remainder of the terrace from Nos. 86–114 down to Chantry Road was completely residential but the final 'front door' held something of a secret, being the entrance to an alleyway leading to a yard behind Nos. 112 and 114.

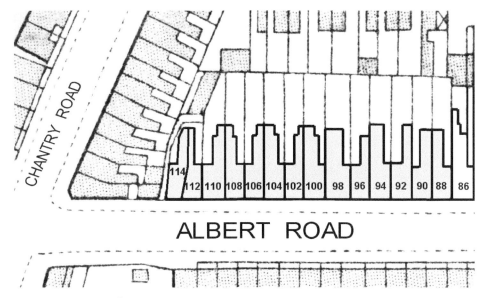

*The southern section of Anderson's Terrace that became Nos. 88–114 Albert Road. A 'hidden' passageway adjacent to No. 114 led to a yard at the rear of the house and its neighbour at No. 112.*

*Nos. 64–78 in Albert Road – originally Anderson's Terrace. No. 64 was a grocer's shop before it became a motor bicycle repair shop (Southampton City Archive).*

# ALBERT ROAD –
## WEST SIDE NOS. 88–114 (ANDERSON'S TERRACE)

*Nos. 92–114 Albert Road. A false 'front door' on the left actually opened into an alleyway that led to a yard behind the houses (Southampton City Archive).*

# ALBERT ROAD –
## NORTH SIDE NOS. 122–126 (ALBERT ROAD SOUTH)

The final southern section of Albert Road from Bridge Terrace to Royal Crescent Road was always named so. After the construction of the Itchen Bridge it became divorced from its northern half and was renamed Albert Road South. This part of the street was home to many seafarers and shipping tradesmen in its early days, mostly in buildings along its southern side, where many of the properties housed several families and lodgers. The north side of the street had few buildings, initially just a couple of public houses and a seamen's mission. The remainder was a recreational open space surrounded by trees and named The Mead.

*The York & Albany stood on the corner of Albert Road and Lower Bridge Road from the 1860s, until its closure in 1972 to make way for the Itchen Bridge. The former Atlantic Hotel can be seen in the distance on the left (Dave Goddard Collection).*

The York and Albany Inn (No. 122) stood on the corner of Lower Bridge Road and dated from the 1860s, with Mrs M. Langdown as one of its earliest licensees. John Smith ran the house for about twenty years from the turn of the century, and William Tizzard was landlord from World War Two until the 1960s. The pub was given a short spell of stardom when scenes for the movie *Stranger in the House* were filmed there in 1966, and it finally closed in 1972.

No. 124 was home to baker Walter Smith in the early 1900s, and the Othen family lived there from the mid-1920s until its demolition in 1967.

No. 126 was another old pub, named the Saracen's Head, which was even older than its near neighbour, dating back to the 1850s. It stood on the corner of Guillaume Terrace. However, it seems to have gone out of business by the late 1880s and became a general shop in the early 1900s. William Bailey was shopkeeper until the 1920s, when Louis Giuliani took over and remained there until the building (known as the Albert Stores) came down in 1973. This former pub also had a resident family in occupation and Charles Taylor was recorded there from 1931 until the shop finally disappeared.

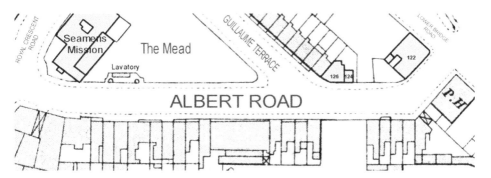

*The southern section of Albert Road ran from Lower Bridge Road to Royal Crescent Road and had very few buildings on its north side.*

Louis Giuliani was single and lived with his sister. At the shop he had an assistant named George, who would ride out on his carrier bike making local deliveries. The shop itself probably never changed much in the half century Louis ran it, with sawdust on the floor and biscuit tins that were constantly topped up but never emptied. The bacon slicer was in constant use with a succession of cooked and raw meats being carved up – but the machine was never cleaned until the end of the day. Winnie the cat was often asleep on the vegetables but despite all this, we customers never seemed to suffer any ill effects. Perhaps we developed immunities!

The only other buildings on the north side of this part of Albert Road were the Missions to Seamen Church & Institute, which is referred to in Royal Crescent Road, and an ancient, roofless urinal that served the open recreation space known as The Mead. This was an asphalted area surrounded by trees that became the haunt of owls at night-time.

# ALBERT ROAD –
# SOUTH SIDE NOS. 123–175 (ALBERT ROAD SOUTH)

The southern side of this section of Albert Road was much more populated than that opposite.

The Royal Albert Hotel (No. 123) stood on the corner of Bridge Terrace and this fine old building, dating back to the 1850s, when James Stratton was the landlord, took its name from Queen Victoria's consort. Early in the 20th century it belonged to Scrace's Star Brewery and was later taken over by Strong's of Romsey. After being closed around 1976,

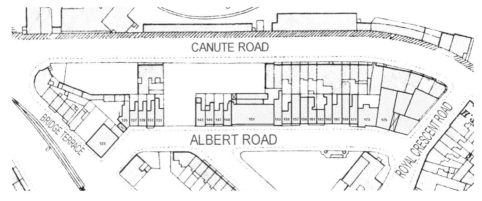

*Albert Road's south side had many more buildings than the opposite side of the street.*

Gales Horndean Brewery took over its final years of operation in 1980, and for many years it was run by Ron and Lyn Ousby before it closed for good in 1998. Having escaped demolition during the building of the Itchen Bridge, it still stands today after conversion to apartments.

No. 125 was, in its early days, another pub with the fanciful name of St Crispin & The Bear, also dating back to the 1850s. The pub ceased trading in 1928 and the building in more recent times became the home of Southampton Social Club and then Southampton Buffs Club. The club served as a great meeting place for friends and families that returned after moving out of the area in the mid-1960s, with stalwarts such as Jackie Wort and Eddie Sparks in regular attendance – along with the odd dockers who were 'between jobs'. However, as many of the old neighbours passed away, the club went into decline and closed

*The northern end of Albert Road South with the Royal Albert Hotel at No. 123 on the corner of Bridge Terrace. No. 125 was originally St Crispin &The Bear, latterly the Southampton Buffs Club.*

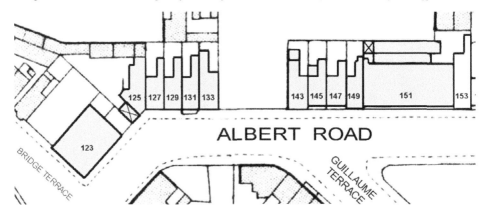

*The Royal Albert Hotel and its neighbour, The Southampton Buffs Social Club, in the 1980s when both were still busy with the local clientele. In the background, between the two, can be seen the former Utility Flats in Canute Road (Dave Marden).*

in 1986. The building was subsequently demolished and rebuilt as social housing, but the facade was retained.

Nos. 127–129 were lodging houses, while No. 131 was another residence and No. 133 was home to several businesses, including a boot polish maker's and a mineral water company. No. 135 was a cold store through to recent times, and No. 143 was always dining rooms before becoming a post-World War Two café. In its later years, it served as a post office after the one in Floating Bridge Road closed, and the building still stands. No. 145 was always a hairdresser's, run for half a century by Miss M. Marshall until it was demolished

*After his passing, a memorial seat was erected to the memory of local resident Jack Wort and placed opposite the Royal Albert and Buffs Club, his regular venues (Steve Marden).*

*The Atlantic Hotel as it was in 1912, being home to many foreign emigrants who sailed to America from Southampton. It later became a labour exchange and is now an apartment block (Dave Marden Collection).*

in the 1950s. Nos. 147 and 149 were residences, while the latter was also a fried fish shop for many years.

No. 151 was the Atlantic Hotel, a stopover for emigrants, mainly on their way to America via the docks. The building also housed a telephone call office at the start of World War One. By the 1930s it had become the Ministry of Labour Employment Exchange and in recent years it was converted into the apartment block that remains today.

*The south side of Albert Road opposite The Mead recreation ground with its row of pubs from Nos. 161–173.*

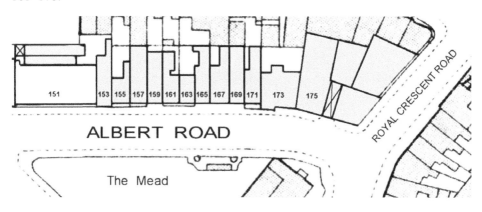

*The bottom end of Albert Road, where it met Royal Crescent Road near the docks, where there was a collection of no less than six consecutive public houses (Dave Goddard Collection).*

No. 153 was at one time used by the British American Tobacco Company in the 1920s, while No. 155 was a butcher's shop in its early days in the 1870s, but then became a grocery shop for the latter part of the 19th century. It then had a spell as a clothier's and outfitter's until it became residential in the 1920s. No. 157 was another residence but No. 159 spent most of its existence as an oil refiner's premises from the turn of the century until becoming a ship stores around 1930, the whole time run by Frank Livett. International Paints shared the premises from the 1930s until the building came down in the 1950s.

The next row of buildings from Nos. 161–173 was an uninterrupted line of pubs with The Alliance Inn, Robert Burns, Welsh Harp, Inkerman Tavern, Calshot Castle and Queens Hotel, all built in the early 1860s. These buildings, originally numbered 48–60, were at the junction with Royal Crescent Road and opposite what was the main dock gate before the early 1900s. Thirsty seamen leaving the docks would be spoiled for choice after a few steps ashore.

The Alliance Inn at No. 161 was run by Mrs Sarah Toogood in its early days until the late 1880s. By the turn of the century, James Darley and his wife Nellie were in charge. The pub was owned by Strongs of Romsey when it closed in 1928, with Mrs Nellie Dennis as its final landlady, and then became a private residence until its demolition.

Next in line was the Robert Burns (at Nos. 163 and 165) owned by Coopers Brewery. Thomas Hall was its early landlord and by the early 1900s it was run by the Davis family. This initially appears to have been two separate buildings with the pub set apart from its next-door dwelling house, but in later years these were merged together with the residence becoming the lounge bar. When entering by the left-hand door it always seemed as though you were walking into someone's living room. The pub was taken over by Watney's in 1940, until becoming a Bass Charrington house in 1978. Robert Fuller was one of the last licensees and closure came in 1980.

At No. 167 stood the Welsh Harp, belonging to Scrace's Brewery. In the 1960s, John Gandy was the landlord and he and his family were in charge for several decades. Mrs Mary Griffin had taken over in the early 1900s until the outbreak of World War One, and William Plowman was the final licensee when it became a café in the 1920s. Named the Milan Café, it remained as such until demolished in the 1980s.

*The Robert Burns in its earlier days as Nos. 50 and 52, a Cooper's Brewery house run by Charles Davis (Dave Marden Collection).*

The Inkerman Inn at No. 169 took its name from the Battle of Inkerman during the Crimean War, and was owned by the Winchester Brewery. During the 1870s the name had changed to the Inkerman Tavern, and it was run by a succession of landlords until it closed in 1915 and became a private residence. By the 1960s it had become the premises of L&G Fire Appliance before it disappeared in that decade.

Forder's Hampton Court Brewery were one-time owners of the Calshot Castle Hotel at No. 171, originally run by William Buers back in the 1860s. By the early 1900s, the word 'Hotel' had been dropped from the name and the pub closed in 1925, afterwards becoming another private residence until it was knocked down in the 1960s.

Last in line of this drinker's paradise was the Queens Hotel at No. 173, which became the final survivor of the row of six pubs. Israel Eden was its landlord in the 1860s and 1870s. After belonging to Aldridge's Bedford Brewery it changed ownership several times, being taken over by Brickwoods, then Whitbread in 1971, before becoming a Bass Charrington

*The Queens Hotel stood between the Calshot Castle and the impressive ships stores of Bell Brothers & Thomson, which was lost in wartime bombing (Dave Marden Collection).*

pub. It survived until comparatively recent times, when it was demolished in haste in the early 2000s to make way for redevelopment and a half-completed block of flats stands in its place, still unfinished after more than a decade.

No. 175 was originally stores for the P&O Shipping Company before becoming Bell Brothers & Thomson Ships Stores around the turn of the century. The building was also occupied by packing manufacturers James Walker & Co. until the building was destroyed by wartime bombing. Walker's later moved to new premises in the adjacent Royal Crescent Road.

# CHAPTER 7.

# *Streets South of Chapel Road*

Streets on the south side of Chapel Road were built in stages. Initially, Paget Street, Nelson Street, Western Terrace and the north side of Anglesea Terrace date from the mid-1840s, but the south side of Anglesea Terrace, and the streets beyond it, were later additions, the area being marshland until around 1870. Albert Road has its own chapter.

## PAGET STREET

Paget Street was one of the earlier residential terraces in Chapel. The houses on the west side were numbered 1–14 from Chapel Road, southwards towards Anglesea Terrace, in 1846. By 1849 the other side of the street was numbered up to 29 in the opposite direction. Nos. 30 and 31 appeared by 1853.

## PAGET STREET – EAST SIDE NOS. 1–15

By 1871 the street had been renumbered, with No. 1 on the east side at the Chapel Road end running south down to Anglesea Terrace, then north again on the west side to No. 31. Further changes incorporated two buildings on the corners at Anglesea Terrace (originally Nos. 10 and 11) which became Nos. 15 and 16 Paget Street respectively.

Using the latter numbering system, we can trace back to the original inhabitants. The site of No. 1 was once that of the P&O School, where the master was Robert Meldrum

*The east side of Paget Street was almost totally destroyed in the Blitz. Only the store at No. 1 and the house at No. 10 survived the bombs.*

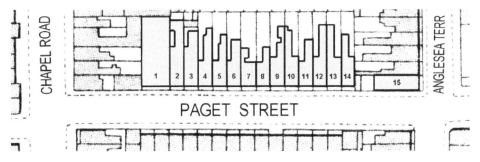

back in 1853. After the school moved to Albert Road around 1875 the site became a potato and fruit merchants in the name of Richard Snook. From the 1840s an adjacent bakehouse existed. This, in its early days, was shown as No. 1 Paget Street but, from the 1920s, became listed under the bakery shop it served at 49 Chapel Road.

A new No. 1 came about in the 1920s when a store was built for Bullivant & Co., who were wire rope makers, until taken over by the firm of British Ropes. In 1939 it was part-occupied by builders Judd and Bulford. By the 1950s, the rope works became Thomas Watkins' Bed Manufacturers premises and by 1960 the building had become Samonas Ships Stores. Its owner, A. J. Samonas, became the Greek Vice-Consulate there around 1975.

No. 2 was occupied by George Grace, who was a sawyer there in 1849 until he became a beer retailer and the premises became the White Lion in 1851. Grace remained behind the bar until the 1870s when his wife Elizabeth succeeded him, until Henry Perring took over in the 1880s. The owners then were the Old Shirley Brewery but the pub belonged to Scrace's Star Brewery when it closed in 1905, with John Ford being the final landlord. It

*No. 10 Paget Street outlived its neighbours who were victims of the Blitz. The vacant spaces on either side were taken up by the Southampton Technical College (Southampton City Archive).*

then became a private residence until, along with most of its neighbours, it was destroyed in World War Two. In fact, No. 10 was the only house standing on the east side of the street after the war.

## PAGET STREET – WEST SIDE NOS. 16–32

On the west side of the street, the original Nos. 1–14 became renumbered 16–32 starting at the Anglesea Terrace end, housing a variety of skilled and professional men and women such as mariners, bootmakers, lath makers, clerks and sail makers during the 1840s to the 1880s.

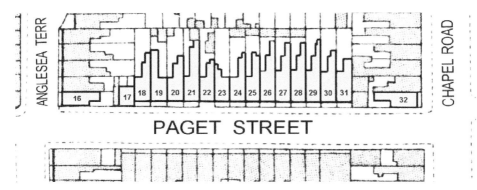

*The west side of Paget Street from Anglesea Terrace to Chapel Road, showing Nos. 16–32.*

No. 17 was at first a private residence until June 1869 when, under the Welsh Lion Brewery, it became the Duke of Edinburgh beer house run by a number of landlords until its closure in 1906. By that time it was in the hands of Welsh's Hyde Brewery and, after it reverted to private residence, the building survived until demolition in the 1960s.

In the 1840s, No. 18 was an eating house run by J. G. Barnes. No. 22 was a general store beginning with Mrs Charlotte Pitt in the 1860s. Harry Giles was in charge there in 1912 and remained so until the 1920s, when the shop closed. Giles remained in residence until the 1930s and the house survived until the 1960s demolition. No. 25 was a dressmaker's run by a Mrs Chiverton and her daughter in the 1870s.

No. 28 was a lodging house run by Mrs Hanna Harvey in 1851, while No. 32 was a greengrocer's from the 1860s until the 1920s, when Mrs Nellie Leigh appears to have

*Looking north along the west side of Paget Street from Anglesea Terrace, with No. 17 on the left of the photo. This was at one time the Duke of Edinburgh pub (Southampton City Archive).*

*The view of Paget Street's west side looking north towards Chapel Road (Southampton City Archive).*

retired from the business and lived there until World War Two, after which Albert Mead took residence in the 1950s and Harold Lawson was the final tenant in 1967.

## NELSON STREET

Nelson Street ran north–south from Chapel Road to Anglesea Terrace, parallel with Paget Street. House Nos. 1–13 ran southwards down the west side and backed on to the main Southampton–London railway line, which ran down to the Terminus Station. Nos. 14–26 were on the east side running north back to Chapel Road. Nos. 27 and 28 appeared in the 1850s, the latter shown as marine stores and a coal dealer.

## NELSON STREET – WEST SIDE NOS. 1–13

The usual bootmakers, mariners and skilled tradesmen were evident. In the 1870s, Mrs Esther Stanton was a dressmaker at No. 6 who had turned to making gas mantles by 1887.

No. 8 was a beer house shown as the White Horse in 1884, but by the 1890s the name had changed to the Nelson Tavern which came under the ownership of Ashby's Eling Brewery until 1922, when Strongs of Romsey took over, holding the licence until it closed in 1930 under the stewardship of Owen Underwood who had been in charge since the Great War. It then became a private residence where the Edwards family lived from 1946 until demolition in 1967.

*The west side of Nelson Street showing Nos. 1–13. No. 8 was once a beer house known firstly as the White Horse and then the Nelson Tavern.*

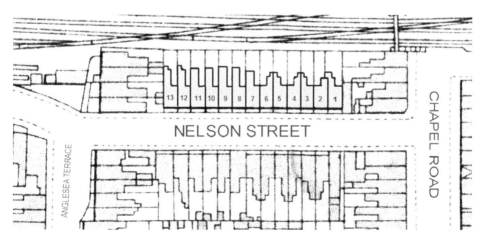

*The west side of Nelson Street viewed from the Chapel Road end (Southampton City Archive).*

## NELSON STREET – EAST SIDE NOS. 14–26

No. 19 was once a pub named the Devonshire Inn. It was first a grocer's shop which began to sell beer in the late 1840s when John Heath was in charge. However, it had closed by

*The east side of Nelson Street showing the pronounced front of No. 19, which was first a shop and then a public house called the Devonshire Inn, which closed in the 1860s.*

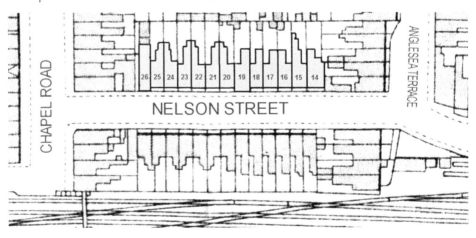

*The east side of Nelson Street looking south from Chapel Road. On the right of the photo can be seen the bay front of what was the former Devonshire Inn at No. 19 (Southampton City Archive).*

the 1860s when Jane Oram ran it. Afterwards, it was just another private residence with the Steer family living there in the post-World War Two period until the street was pulled down in 1967.

*Another view of the east side of Nelson Street, looking north from Anglesea Terrace with the former Devonshire Inn just visible behind the van. The distant chimney is in the gasworks, to the north of Chapel Road (Southampton City Archive).*

# WESTERN TERRACE

Western Terrace was situated south of Chapel Road on the west side of the railway that ran down to the Terminus Station. Houses occupied only the east side of the street, while the land opposite, once an orchard, became Deanery School in 1930. The corner premises was No. 1, which in some directories appeared as No. 65 Chapel Road, and throughout its time was a grocer's shop, fruit merchant's and a second-hand furniture store. Twelve more houses then formed a line down to No. 13. Five more dwellings, Nos. 14–19, then turned off eastwards at right angles, ending alongside the railway. The end house, No. 19, housed railway employees until it was removed in the mid-1880s to allow widening of the railway, and a turntable for locomotives was installed by South Western Railway to the south of Nos. 14–18. In fact, during the 1880s several of the Western Terrace houses were occupied by railway personnel with guards, inspectors and police in residence. Other residents in the mid-1880s included shipwrights, clerks, a nurse and a vat builder. Of long-term residents, Rueben Lane, a railway police inspector, lived at No. 16 from the 1880s until the 1920s. Harry Savage was at No. 15 from around 1912 until the outbreak of World War Two. James Littlejohn moved into that address after the war and was one of the final residents when the street came down. The Thompson family were also one of the last, having been at No. 11 since the 1920s.

As the Terminus Station fell into decline in the 1960s, the abandoned turntable became a favourite playground for the local youngsters in turning the handles and moving the

*Western Terrace was a cul-de-sac that ran from Chapel Road, ending with gate to the railway yard north of the Terminus Station.*

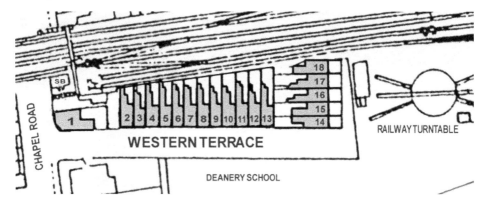

contraption like a giant roundabout. Like many of its neighbours, Western Terrace was removed around 1965. Deanery School was closed in 1989 and the site was redeveloped as flats.

## ANGLESEA TERRACE

Like many other Chapel streets, Anglesea Terrace saw house numbers change as the area developed, but most retained their original identities. The buildings on the corners of Paget Street were originally Nos. 11 and 9 in the terrace, but were later 'moved' into the Paget Street numbers. Of the others, Nos. 1–10 on the east of the terrace were always so, while the middle section between Paget and Nelson Streets were all 'moved up one' in the numerical order to become Nos. 11–19. The same applied to the remaining four houses at the western end adjacent to the railway. These were known as Upper Anglesea Terrace in the 1840s.

## ANGLESEA TERRACE – NORTH SIDE NOS. 1–23

The northern side of Anglesea Terrace was built long before its southern side was developed. This marked the limit of Chapel's southern expansion in the 1840s, and the opposite side of the street came some 30 years later.

No. 1 was originally a house but became a pub in the 1840s, named the Royal Standard. It was run in those days by George Bowles and owned by the Cobden Bridge Brewery. By

*Anglesea Terrace was in three sections numbered from east to west with Nos. 1 and 2 becoming the Anglesea Tavern on the corner of Albert Road.*

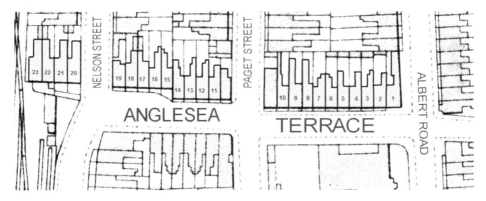

the 1870s, Thomas Blewden was in charge, selling groceries as well as beer until around the turn of the century when the name was changed to the Anglesea Tavern under new owners, the Fuller, Smith and Turner's Brewery. It changed hands again in November 1920 when purchased by the Courage Brewery, who rebuilt and extended it, taking over its neighbour at No. 2. The 'new' building had three bars: the Public Bar, with its door on the corner; the Lounge Bar, entered from Albert Road; and the Games Bar, with its door on Anglesea Terrace. There was also a Bottle and Jug counter between the public and lounge bars.

In 1948 the pub had a celebrated visitor. Tagart, Morgan & Cole had a timber yard near the Anglesea Tavern in Ryde Terrace where George the horse was employed and, on that famous occasion, his handler Fred Millard led him into the public bar for a Christmas drink, and a photograph of the event hung on the wall for 40 years afterwards.

Despite all the upheavals and obliteration of Chapel, and a period of closure, the Anglesea remains to this day as the sole survivor of all the Chapel pubs and, after a couple of changes of name, is now the Chapel Arms.

*The Anglesea Tavern after the neighbouring houses had been demolished in the 1960s. It remains to this day as the sole survivor of all the Chapel pubs and, after a couple of changes of name, is now the Chapel Arms (Dave Goddard Collection).*

*George the horse joining in the fun in the Anglesea Tavern public bar at Christmas time in 1948. Handler Fred Millard is seen by his side, with his brother behind them (Courtesy Bill Millard).*

*Of all the scores of pubs around Chapel's streets, only one remains. The former Anglesea Tavern is now the Chapel Arms (Dave Marden).*

*Anglesea Terrace from right to left, with the Anglesea Tavern as Nos. 1 and 2 with Nos. 3–5 shown. Nos. 6–10 were victims of wartime bombing (Southampton City Archive).*

*The corner of Anglesea Terrace and Nelson Street showing, from left to right, Nos. 19–15 that were set back from the rest of the terrace. Nos. 14–10 are visible on the far right (Southampton City Archive).*

*The final western section of Anglesea Terrace was four houses numbered 20–23 (Southampton City Archive).*

Back in the 1950s, three generations of my family lived almost opposite the Anglesea Tavern at our house in Albert Road, and I have childhood memories of my grandmother shuffling across the street to the Bottle and Jug Bar which was the middle door facing onto Albert Road. It was not really a bar but just a passageway leading to a counter with a bench seat down one side. Gran would call in there sometimes twice nightly for a pint of half and half (mild and bitter), collected in her china jug which she would take back home and place on the kitchen range in her room. The heat would bring the beer to her desired temperature, and one evening she asked me, 'Would you like to try a drop?' As an innocent young boy I thought this must taste wonderful, so I was quite shocked to gulp down a mouthful of this warm and bitter liquid. To me it tasted vile – but I have grown quite accustomed to the taste since then, although I do prefer it much cooler!

## ANGLESEA TERRACE – SOUTH SIDE NOS. 24–30

Whereas the north side of Anglesea Terrace appeared in the early years of Chapel's being, the south side of the street remained as open land until around 1870, when buildings began to spread down towards the docks.

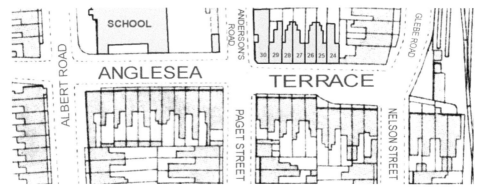

*The south side of Anglesea Terrace had just six houses and a grocery shop, the rest being taken up by the local school.*

Nos. 24–30 were between Anderson's Road and Glebe Road, and appeared on the street directories around that date with a collection of policemen, storekeepers and shoemakers in residence. No. 30 on the corner of Anderson's Road was always a grocery shop with a long line of proprietors, ending with W. J. Feltham when it closed prior to demolition in 1966.

*No. 30 Anglesea Terrace was a grocery shop on the corner of Anderson's Road. It is pictured here in 1918 when Thomas Cox was the proprietor (Dave Marden Collection).*

*Looking east along the south side of Anglesea Terrace, where numbers 24–30 are shown on the left of the photo by the Mini. The Eastern District School is beyond them. The building on the corner of Glebe Road on the right is the former Myrtle public house (Southampton City Archive).*

The remainder of the south side of the street was taken up by the Eastern District School, formerly run by the P&O Shipping Company for its employees' children (see Albert Road chapter).

# CHAPTER 8.

## Streets South of Anglesea Terrace

Many further streets were added to the Chapel area from around 1870, and these included Anderson's Road, Glebe Road and Chantry Road.

### ANDERSON'S ROAD

Anderson's Road appeared in the second building phase of Chapel streets, when development of the marshlands to the south of Anglesea Terrace began in the late 1860s. The first list of residents is shown in the 1871 directory, and is remarkable for the large number of engineers living there, twelve in total with many other professional grades including four pilots. In the directories of the 1870s, not one resident is listed as a labourer. Almost as noteworthy is the fact that Anderson's Road was one of the few Chapel streets of any stature not to have its own pub. Not even a beer house appears throughout its history, although the Gurney Arms did stand on the corner of its junction with Chantry Road.

Several properties in the street had cottage names in the 1870s. On the west side, No. 7 was Waterloo House, No. 10 was Tyne Cottage, No. 13 St Hilda's Cottage, 17 Wilts Cottage and 24 Gower Cottage.

*The west side of Anderson's Road, showing Nos. 1–25. Some of the houses at the Chantry Road end were of three storeys.*

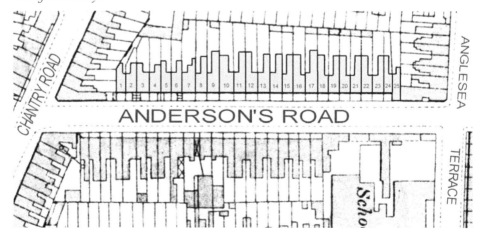

*The west side of Anderson's Road looking south from Anglesea Terrace, with demolition of No. 25 already in progress (Dave Marden Collection).*

*Another view of the west side of Anderson's Road taken from the roof of the former Eastern District School in the 1960s, when demolition had already begun in Chantry Road. The photo illustrates the different styles of housing, with some buildings being three storeys with a basement (Dave Marden Collection).*

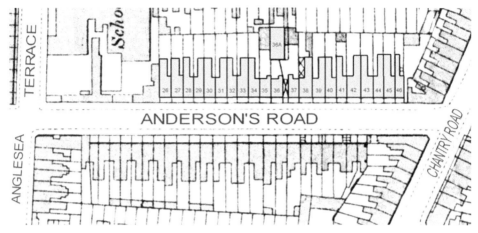

*The east side of Anderson's Road, showing Nos. 26–46. No. 36A was a yard with workshops reached by an alleyway between Nos. 36 and 37.*

Nos. 1–4 were the first houses to go in the 1960s clearance programme, disappearing from the directories after 1964 and, after 1940, the only resident shown at No. 25 was a Mrs M. Le-Sauvage in 1954.

*The east side of Anderson's Road, showing Nos. 27–41. In the distant left is the former Eastern District School. Again evident are the three-storey houses at Nos. 35–38, with the alleyway entrance to 36A between Nos. 36 and 37 (Southampton City Archive).*

*The east side of Anderson's Road at its southern end, showing Nos. 39–46 (Southampton City Archive).*

The east side of Anderson's Road was as much of a mixture as the houses opposite, with some larger buildings of three storeys and others named as cottages. No. 26 was Kent Cottage, 27 Transit Cottage, 28 Myrtle Cottage and 29 Rose Cottage. For some reason, No. 37 appears to have been uninhabited between 1931 and 1954. The Small or Smale family occupied No. 45, from 1876 right through continuously until 1948.

Between Nos. 36 and 37 an alleyway led to a cobbled yard that contained several small businesses over the years. The first mention is of the Southern Engineering Company, who were electrical engineers there in 1912. In the 1920s, the Torbay Paint Company had stores there along with the ship's finishing works of H. J. Burgess. In the 1930s, sheet metal workers L. Young and Co. were there. Seymour Smith & Co. occupied the premises from 1939 until the mid-1960s. They were lubricating oil and grease manufacturers, a business that was taken over by Butler Chemicals in the final couple of years before the street came down.

Anderson's Road proved to be one of the last streets to hang on, until it finally succumbed to the bulldozers in 1967. After the houses were all gone, the vast open area left behind became a series of lorry parks, with Pitter Brothers and the Sibley Group using the space until the new flats and houses sprung up in the 2000s.

## GLEBE ROAD

Glebe Road was parallel with Anderson's Road and, likewise, ran from Anglesea Terrace to Chantry Road. The houses stood only on the east side of the street, as opposite was a boundary wall along the main railway line to the Terminus Station.

No. 1 was a pub called The Myrtle, although in earlier days it was named the Oddfellows Arms, having changed its name in the 1880s. The Harding family ran the pub from around the turn of the century almost until its closure in 1932, when it became just a residence.

*The former Myrtle pub on the corner of Glebe Road and Anglesea Terrace had long been a private residence when this photo was taken in the 1960s (Southampton City Archive).*

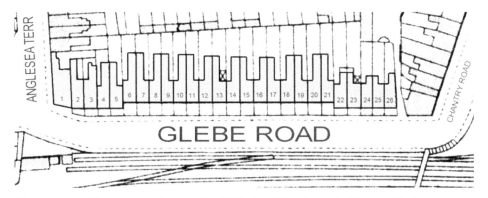

*The single row of houses along the east side of Glebe Road. No. 1 was the Myrtle public house which closed in 1932 and became an ordinary residence.*

The houses at Nos. 2–5 and 22–26 at either end if the street were larger buildings than the ones in between. The Ford family resided continuously at No. 12 from the early 1900s until 1960. No. 13 was occupied by master mariner and one-time tugboat captain Henry Cockett from the 1880s until the 1920s. Other long-term occupants were the Sims family,

*Nos. 4–21 Glebe Road looking south from the Anglesea Terrace towards Chantry Road – with a distinct lack of parked cars (Southampton City Archive).*

who lived at No. 21 from the end of World War Two until the street's final days in 1966, as did the Murray family next door at No. 22.

No. 26, at the bottom of the road, became home to a number of businesses operating from a yard at its rear. Potato merchants Challis & Quinn were there in the 1920s, until Edward Louis & Co. set up a motor garage there in the 1930s. Leonard Roberts took over the business in the post-World War Two years and the final occupants were the Glebe Sheet Metal Works in the 1950s.

At the bottom end of the street was a footbridge that spanned the adjacent railway, and on the corner of Chantry Road stood the Freemans Arms.

## CHANTRY ROAD

Chantry Road is one of those streets that evolved from a series of individual terraces, but came into its own around the turn of the 20th century when it stretched from Glebe Road all the way down to Dock Street and Floating Bridge Road. The north side was fairly uncomplicated but the south side had several identities before it became 'joined up' with its opposite neighbours. Not to say that the north side was without its changes, and the odd mystery.

At its peak, the odd numbers 1–77 ran along the north side in four sections from Glebe Road to Dock Street, with No. 1 (the Freeman's Arms) to 27 (the Gurney Arms) making up the first section between Glebe Road and Anderson's Road. Then from Anderson's Road to Albert Road the numbers ran 29–53. Continuing from Albert Road to Ryde Terrace as Nos. 55–65 and, finally, 67–77 from Ryde Terrace to Dock Street.

It is rather strange that most of Nos. 31–51 between Anderson's Road and Albert Road do not appear in the directories from 1907–16, although Nos. 31–33 are shown in 1907. Another oddity was the shape of the houses from Nos. 8–25 and Nos. 45–51. These all had their rear extensions at an angle to the main building. This was no doubt to compensate for the alignment of neighbouring streets but seems an odd piece of planning.

The original buildings on the north side were numbered 1–14 from Glebe Road to Anderson's Road, then 15–27 between Anderson's Road and Albert Road. The terrace between Albert Road and Ryde Terrace was previously named Queen's Road and numbered

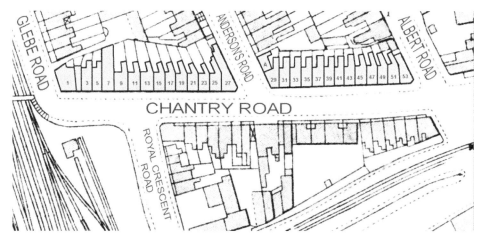

*The north side of Chantry Road with Nos. 1–53 between Glebe Road and Albert Road in 1910. Nos. 55–77 continued between Albert Road and Dock Street. The building between Nos. 1 and 3 was originally No. 2, until it became part of the Freeman's Arms.*

1–12, running from Albert Road to Dock Street. Queen's Road became part of Chantry Road around the turn of the century when renumbered 55–77.

To look more closely at Chantry Road and understand its make up, it is probably easier to break it into several sections. The north side from Glebe Road to Albert Road, then Albert Road to Dock Street (the former Queen's Road), then on the south side from Royal Crescent to Albert Road. For familiarity, the later odd and even numbers are shown and references to previous terraces and numbers are added.

The north side of Chantry Road began with No. 1 the Freeman's Arms, which appeared in the 1871 directory with the landlord Henry Edmead listed as Builder & Innkeeper. It belonged to the Winchester Brewery in early days but was taken over by Marston's, who owned the pub when it closed in 1966. My own recollection of this place was that it was quite spartan with bare floorboards and a clientele that perhaps were unwelcome in the many neighbouring hostelries, with rough cider being a speciality of the house.

The next-door premises (originally No. 2) was once an eating house and later became absorbed as part of the pub. No. 7 was always a shop, once run by the Bignell family in the 1880s, but the grocer's had a variety of hosts before it became a hairdresser's before World War One when run by John Masters, and seems to have ceased being a business premises after the war. No. 9 was a greengrocer's until after World War Two, when it changed to

*The Freeman's Arms on the corner of Chantry and Glebe Roads, glimpsed through the steam from a passing train in the 1930s (Dave Marden Collection).*

general groceries. The Strange family ran it from the early 1900s, until Mrs Rosie Cook took over in the 1950s and remained in charge until the street came down in 1966.

No. 11 was a furniture dealer's, run by Mrs Croucher in pre-World War One days, and No. 17 was once a lodging house around the turn of the century. The Crouchman family lived at No. 19 from around 1890 until World War One. Another long-term resident was Mrs Alice Murphy, who ran No. 23 as a lodging house back in 1911. She stayed in residence until the mid-1920s. No. 25 was another shop that hosted various businesses in its time, until it appears to have ceased trading by the mid-1930s.

On the corner of Chantry Road and Anderson's Road stood No. 27, the Gurney Arms, which hailed from the same period at The Freeman's Arms along the street. When the streets were cleared in the mid-1960s, the Gurney closed in 1965 but had a remarkable reprieve (albeit briefly) the following year when MGM used it for scenes in a film they were

*The Gurney Arms had a brief reprieve and a moment of stardom before it finally fell to the bulldozers (Dave Goddard Collection).*

making with James Mason and Geraldine Chaplin. Titled *Stranger in the House,* the film also featured the nearby York and Albany in Albert Road and several local streets.

On the opposite corner, across Anderson's Road, stood No. 29, which was once a baker's, then a sweet shop, but mostly traded as a grocer's from the 1880s until 1940. Robert Grant ran the business from 1911–39. No. 53 was firstly a pork butcher's shop in the 1880s, then a fried fish shop in 1907, but by 1911 it had become the boot-making premises of Ernest Spagagna until 1940. After World War Two, the Sakkas family ran it as a grocery shop until that part of the street came down around 1960.

Something of a mystery surrounds the terrace of houses numbered 31–51. None of these houses appear in the street directories from 1907–16, although there is a solitary entry for Mrs Baker at No. 33 in 1912. They all are included in the 1911 census but nothing more is recorded in the directories until 1920, after which normality returns until the 1930s when, once again, the houses go 'missing' with only occasional entries for the Stride family at No. 33, the Joneses at No. 43 and the Parsons family at No. 51. It is not until the

*Burrough's Pork Butchers shop on the corner of Chantry Road and Albert Road, which was one of several businesses housed in that building over its lifetime (Dave Marden Collection).*

*The buildings from Albert Road to Dock Street were originally named Queen's Road, but became an extension of Chantry Road around the turn of the 20th century. Originally numbered 1–12 Queen's Road, they became Nos. 55–77 Chantry Road. This street was also the tram terminus for services to the nearby floating bridge.*

1950s that any general occupants are shown in that row of houses, which finally came down around 1960.

The former Queen's Road, at what was the foot of the Central Bridge, was numbered 1–12 until it became an extension of Chantry Road around the turn of the 20th century, and took the numbers 55–77. No. 55, on the corner of Albert Road, was a grocery shop, as was No. 67 on the corner of Ryde Terrace. These and the buildings in between them were destroyed in the Blitz, but newsagent Joseph Reeves-Rowland continued there in temporary premises after the war until the 1950s.

No. 69 began as a general shop but became a butcher's, and then a fishmonger's around World War One run by the Wake family for a couple of decades up to about 1950. No. 71 was also a butcher's shop and stayed as such until the 1950s when Percy Kelly ran the business. No. 73 was originally two buildings, a general store and a greengrocer's, which were merged into one. No. 75 was for many years also a business premises when, in the 1880s, it was a hairdresser's, then an umbrella maker's before becoming a bootmaker's shop. Mrs Sage took over as a wardrobe dealer around 1914 and remained as such until the bombs fell in 1940. No. 77 was a general shop in the 1880s but became a hairdresser's in the early 1900s, and was run by Albert Norton from 1911 until the outbreak of World War Two. Only the buildings at Nos. 67, 69 and 71 survived the war but were swept away when the area was cleared in the 1950s.

*A tram at the Queen's Road terminus (latterly Chantry Road). On the left can be seen the buildings between Ryde Terrace and Dock Street with Wakes fishmongers (No. 69) and Kelly's butchers (No. 71) showing post-war bomb damage (Bert Moody Collection).*

*The south side of Chantry Road in 1910, where Nos. 40–30 were originally Nos. 1–6 Vulcan Terrace, which also included Nos. 7 and 8 (12 and 14), with No. 1 (40) being the Vulcan Tavern. Nos. 22–28 were referred to as Improved Dwellings, having been converted into 16 flats. Nos. 2–10 were formerly known as 1–5 Cherville Terrace.*

*The Vulcan Tavern stood at the junction of Chantry Road and Central Bridge. This, and the houses behind it, originally formed Vulcan Terrace (Dave Marden Collection).*

The buildings on the south side of Chantry Road were far more complicated than those across the street. Latterly, the numbers ran as evens from No. 2 at the Royal Crescent Road end to No. 40 at the junction with Albert Road, where No. 40 was the Vulcan Tavern. This had earlier marked the beginning of Vulcan Terrace, numbered 1–8 in the opposite direction with the pub being No. 1. At that time, Nos. 2–6 ran immediately westwards from the Vulcan Tavern, but Nos. 7 and 8 appear to have been further up the street, where they eventually became Nos. 12 and 14 under the new scheme (No. 16 appeared around the turn of the century when it was listed as a furniture dealer's).

Next to No. 6 Vulcan Terrace were four blocks of flats, numbered 1–16 (latterly Nos 22-28) under the title of *Improved Dwellings*, later appearing as *The Flats – Model Dwellings*. The buildings at the Royal Crescent Road end (latterly 2–10) were formerly listed as Cherville Terrace Nos. 1–5. The Vulcan Tavern closed in the 1950s but the building remained empty and then became a store, before finally being demolished in the 1960s, which also saw the end of the nearby flats.

*A stunning aerial photo taken in the 1920s shows Chantry Road running from bottom left of the picture, and includes the former Queen's Road terrace in the centre where a tram approaches Central Bridge. To the right of the tram is the Royal Albert Hotel on the corner of Albert Road (Dave Marden Collection).*

There is a curious note in the 1884 directory that mentions Chantry Road as '*now named March Lane*', but this name does not appear in any other directory either before or afterwards. This is probably due to Chantry Road once being a continuation of Marsh Lane before having its own identity.

# CHAPTER 9.

## Roads East of Albert Road

Chapel suffered its share of wartime bombing, but the area east of Albert Road, built mainly in the 1870s, was pretty well decimated during the Blitz air raids of 1940 and 1941. The Supermarine factory, building Spitfire planes on the opposite bank of the River Itchen, was a prime target for enemy bombers. Very little was left of this corner of Chapel when the wartime destruction was cleared away. Although the west side of Elm Street remained partly intact, very little was left of its east side, which together with Elm Road, Wharf Street, Endle Street, Dock Street, Deal Street and Crosshouse Road were practically obliterated.

## ELM STREET

Elm Street was tucked away behind Albert Road and ran from Dock Street to Chapel Road. It began as a small group of houses in the 1860s known as Elm Place, numbered 1–6. This site was previously occupied by Elm Cottage and its gardens and the 'new' terrace was later absorbed into Elm Street, which was then numbered Nos. 25–15 in the opposite direction as the street grew in the 1880s. Along its course (to add to the confusion) were Elm Terrace and Elm Road.

The west side of Elm Street had an industrial site on the corner of Elm Terrace, where No. 11 was a blacksmith's shop run by Walter Hookey from the 1930s. There were also several haulage firms based there, as well as a fishmonger, a grocer and a bootmaker at No. 13A.

Strangely, there was a break in the odd numbers and there is no trace of Nos. 31–35, which may have been industrial premises in the gap between Nos. 29 and 37. One of the longest-serving residents was Frank Rio, who lived in No. 23 from the early 1900s until that part of the street (Nos. 11–25) was destroyed by bombing in 1940. Nos. 27–45 survived the war but were demolished with the rest of the street in the 1950s. The top end of the street towards Chapel Road had various stores and yards associated with the nearby wharf.

*The building that stood on the corner of Elm Terrace was No. 13, and at one time No. 13A on the left was a bootmaker's shop before World War Two. In the yard behind was No. 11, the home of various industries including a blacksmith (Southampton City Archive).*

*The west side of Elm Street with Nos. 11–45 showing the space between Nos. 29 and 37. Nos. 15–25 were originally known as Elm Place.*

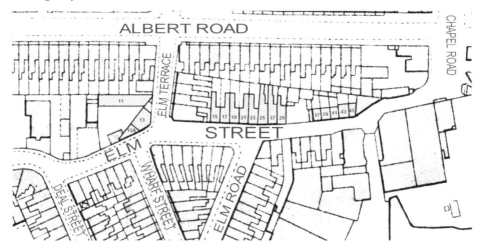

The east side of Elm Street was more populated, with houses in three groups having even numbers 2–40. The first section between Deal Street and Wharf Street was Nos. 2–12, which first appeared in the 1880s. No. 2 on the corner of Deal Street was always a general shop right from the beginning, until it was destroyed in World War Two, but this was the exception because all the others in this row survived the war until they were demolished in the 1950s. The Aikman family lived at No. 4 from the 1880s until the 1930s, likewise, John Sawyer was another long-term resident who lived at No. 10 from the early 1900s until 1940.

Some of the houses in Elm Street were very small and had front doors that opened directly into the living room. I remember one Welsh family that lived there with quite a few children that often played outside in bare feet.

Nos. 14–28 between Wharf Street and Elm Road were all lost to German bombing. This group of eight houses formed one side of a triangle of streets that led to the Corporation Yard. No. 14 was a grocer's shop on the corner of Wharf Street. No. 22 was occupied by Frederick Whitfield from around 1912 until 1940, while Jeremiah Eversley lived at No. 24 between the wars.

*Local children gathered for the photographer in Elm Street pre-World War One, doing their best to look interested. Even the parrot seems ill at ease (Dave Marden Collection).*

*Above and opposite top right, two views of the old Millers House at ChapelWharf photographed in 1941, possibly after bomb damage (both Southampton City Archive).*

*Opposite right, the east side of Elm Street showing even Nos. 2–40 in three groups.*

The final section north of Elm Road began with No. 30, where the Kean family lived from around 1912 until the very end. This house was separated from No. 32 by an alleyway leading to the rear of the Isle of Wight Co. engineering works and the British American Tobacco Co. warehouse at Chapel Wharf. Spencer Harrison lived at No. 38 from the beginning of World War One until the house was destroyed in 1940.

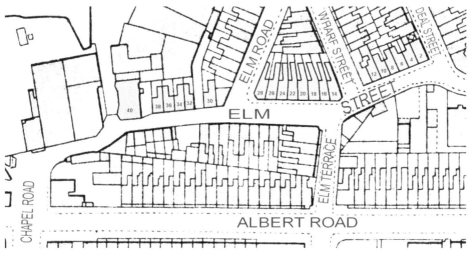

No. 40 was a large detached building at one time known as Chapel House. Built in 1740 on the site of the old Trinity Church, it was attached to the local tide mill and known as the Miller's House until the mid-1800s, when it was used by several commercial firms, including the Anglo-American Oil Co. who were oil cake manufacturers in the 1920s. From the mid-1920s, the building appears to have been let as two dwellings that were inhabited until vacated in the war, after which the building became derelict and was demolished in 1960.

At the northern end of Elm Street was the entrance to Chapel Wharf and the American Wharf. In 1871 the St Mary's Steam Saw Mill was evident at Chapel Wharf, but didn't last very long. There was also Westlake's Corn Merchants along with firewood merchants Robert Burnett & Co. In the early 1900s, auctioneers Southern Counties Trading Society were there until around the 1920s, when the British American Tobacco Co. moved in. Their warehouse was destroyed by bombs in World War Two. In the 1950s, the Isle of Wight Stream Packet Co., better known as Red Funnel Ferries, set up engineering workshops there. While at the adjacent American Wharf, corn merchants Fear Colebrook & Co. occupied the ancient warehouse which still stands today. It was built in 1838 and the Colebrook Company was there from the early 1900s through to the 1950s, when E. Mayes & Son (later Owen Owen) moved in.

Further along, the town corporation had sewage works and an incinerator, and these are shown under Elm Road.

## ELM ROAD

Elm Road ran from Elm Street to the old Corporation Wharf near Crosshouse. It was built early in the 20th century and contained a row of 11 houses, along with the main entrance to the Corporation Yard, where there was a sewage works and an incinerator along with a few commercial occupants. Inside the yard was also a works cottage, at one time occupied by horse keeper Richard Taylor during the First World War and into the 1920s. Leslie Chalk was another occupant prior to World War Two.

Of the 11 houses, 10 were in a terrace along the north side of the street and No. 11 was on the corner of Elm Street. All were destroyed in the wartime bombing except for No. 7, where the Early family remained until around 1948.

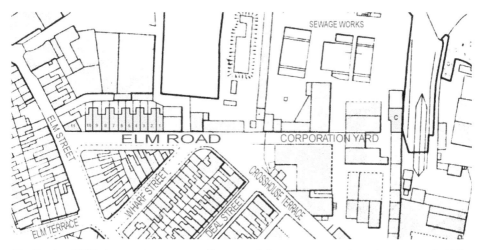

*Elm Road in 1910, showing the main row of houses and the corporation works yard cottage marked 'C'.*

# ELM TERRACE

Situated between Albert Road and Elm Street, Elm Terrace was probably the shortest and least populated of all the Chapel streets, comprising just three houses and a pub on its northern side.

*The former Shipwright's Arms on the corner of Elm Terrace and Elm Street. The full extent of Elm Terrace being the pub and the three houses to its left (Southampton City Archive).*

*Elm Street children seemed popular with photographers. This gathering was grouped outside the Shipwright's Arms (Dave Marden Collection).*

*The buildings of Elm Terrace tucked away between Albert Road and Elm Street.*

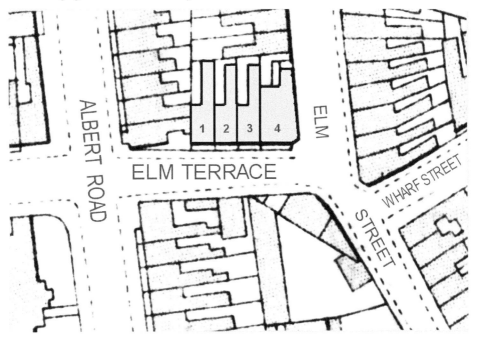

The Shipwrights Arms at No. 4 was also known as the Joiner's Arms back in 1871, possibly due to its landlord being one George Joyner (who happened to be a shipwright), and was owned by Barlow's Victoria Brewery. Previously its address had been No. 6 Elm Place until the 1880s, then, sometime around the outbreak of World War One, another change of identity saw it become No. 15 Elm Street. The pub was refused a licence in 1924 when James V. Booth was in charge. That address was then listed as Walter Hannan's fried fish shop in the 1930s, until, with many of the surrounding properties, it was destroyed by wartime bombing.

## WHARF STREET

Wharf Street formed one side of a triangular block of three streets – the other two being Elm Street and Elm Road. The houses on the north side of Wharf Street were built at an angle to the road and gradually diminished in size the nearer they got to the corner of Elm Road. In the earlier directories, these were known as Crouch's (or Crouches) Buildings and numbered 1–5, but later became odd numbers 1–9 when the street was renumbered. Like many other streets in the area, Wharf Street was a victim of enemy bombing in World War Two when all the houses on the north side were destroyed. Cornelius Day lived at No.

*Odd numbers 1–9 on the north side of Wharf Street were once known as Crouch's Buildings.*

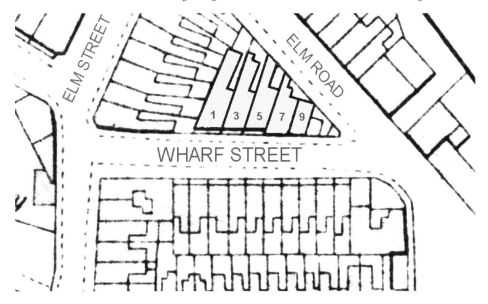

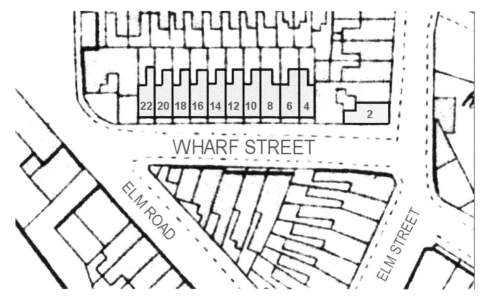

*The south side of Wharf Street. Nos. 2–14 survived the war but were cleared away in the 1950s.*

5 from the early 1900s until his home was lost in the Blitz. Likewise, the Lawrence family lived at No. 9 from World War One until 1940.

The south side of Wharf Street was more populated with 11 dwellings, with even Nos. 2–22 running east from Elm Street. No. 2 was once known as Perseverance Cottage. There was also an annex as No. 2A which appears to have been workshops or stores at the rear of the building. The Wilkins family lived at No. 8 from around 1911 until the street came down in the mid-1950s. William Taylor resided at No. 20 from the early 1900s, until Nos. 16–22 were lost in the air raids. After the war, the remainder of the street was demolished in the mid-1950s.

## DEAL STREET

Deal Street was originally named Dock Terrace and ran from the north end of Dock Street to Crosshouse Terrace. It was presumably named in association with the large timber yard adjacent to it. It rose up a slight incline to the corporation yard's incinerator and was known locally as 'Burner Hill'. The numbers ran consecutively, on the south side from No. 1 (actually in Dock Street) along to No. 17, then back again on the north side from 18–30.

*The Dock Tavern, long since shut when photographed in 2016, with what remains of Deal Street on the left (Dave Marden).*

The south side of Deal Street was known as Dock Terrace until the mid-1880s. No. 2, The Dock Tavern, stood on the corner of Dock Street.

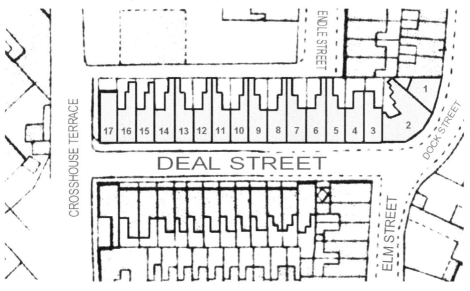

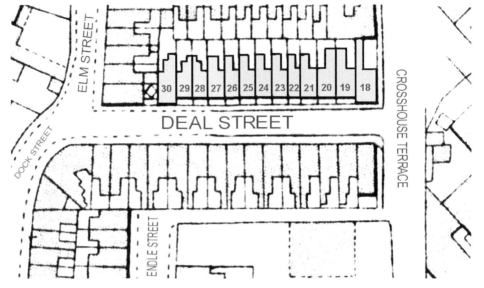

*The north side of Deal Street showing Nos. 18–30.*

Until the 1880s, only the south side existed – apart from No. 18, which was then the sole residence on the other side of the road. When the north side was completed in the 1880s, Nos. 24 and 25 were named Cedar Cottage and Myrtle Cottage respectively.

No. 2 was the Dock Tavern dating from the early 1870s when James Ford was the innkeeper. In the early 1900s, the pub was owned by Ashby's Eling Brewery and William Patterson was behind the bar until the 1920s. It was taken over by Strongs of Romsey and rebuilt in their mock Tudor style during the 1930s, when Norman Britton became landlord until the outbreak of World War Two, after which the pub continued trading until 1961 when it became the offices of the Boilermakers' Trade Union. Strong's builders did a fine job as it was the only building in Deal Street to survive the wartime bombing raids, and the rebuilt Dock Tavern is now the only reminder of the past in that street.

Albert Fanstone was one of Deal Street's longest-sitting tenants, living at No. 7 from around 1912 until the street was lost.

## RYDE TERRACE

Ryde Terrace ran north to south from Dock Street to the section of Chantry Road that was formerly Queen's Road, with houses only on its eastern side. Beginning with No. 1 at the

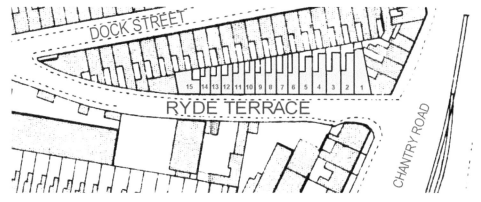

*Ryde Terrace in 1910, showing the single row of houses on the eastern side.*

southern end, the numbers ran consecutively to 15 with a store next door. The opposite side of the street was occupied by commercial premises including a timber yard, coal merchant and an iron foundry.

The earliest list of residents appeared in the 1871 directory and John Broomfield was one of the early long-standing tenants, living at No. 4 from 1884–1920. The Hitchings family resided at No. 5 from 1912–40 while Victor Jolliffe also appeared in directories at No. 6 from 1907–20. Ryde Terrace also saw several other inhabitants living in the street for very long periods.

The Dowdings were at No. 12 from 1907–35, where head of the house Henry earned a living as a wood bundle maker back in 1911. Despite the wartime bombing, most of the houses, from Nos. 4–14, survived until they were finally cleared away in the mid-1950s.

## DOCK STREET

Dock Street ran north to south from Deal Street to Crosshouse Road and, with over 50 houses, was one of the more populated streets in Chapel. Sadly, it fared much worse than its neighbours during World War Two, when it was reduced to just three houses left in occupation after hostilities ceased.

Unlike many other Chapel Streets that saw a huge turnover of residents over the years, Dock Street residents seemed fairly content to remain there for most of their lives. The Hall family lived at No. 1 from the early 1900s until the 1930s, while neighbours at No. 2 were

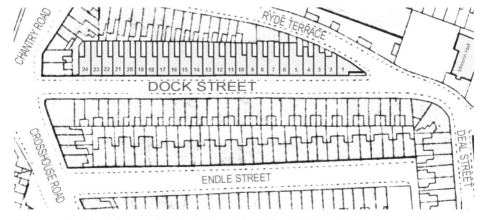

*The west side of Dock Street with Nos. 1–24 and the St Mary's Mission Hall opposite Deal Street.*

the Meills who occupied from the same period, right through until the street was lost in the Blitz. Likewise, the Catchloves were in No. 5 for a similar time.

No. 7 is listed as a beer house run by Henry Tubbs in the 1880s, but after the turn of the century it became a general shop under William Smith until Thomas Fanstone took

*The old Mission Hall facing Dock Street is one of the few original Chapel buildings still evident (Dave Marden).*

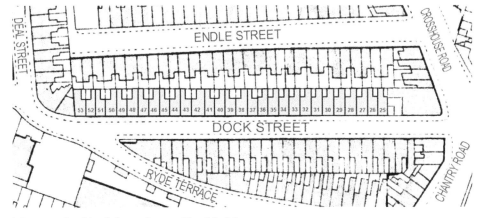

*The west side of Dock Street showing Nos. 25–53*

over in the 1920s. Nos. 8, 9 and 10 were the only survivors after the war, occupied by George Sketcher, Mrs Sims and William Gale respectively when the street was finally cleared in the mid-1950s. John Payne resided at No. 11 from the early 1900s until the wartime bombing, while dressmaker Mrs Eliza lived at No. 15 for most of the first quarter of the 20th century. No. 17 was home to the Riddett family from the early 1900s until 1940.

In the 1880s, St Mary's Mission Room was set up almost opposite the junction with Deal Street and became a popular Sunday school for local children in the 1950s. It is one of the few original Chapel buildings still standing but has long been used for commercial purposes.

The occupants of Nos. 25–53 were no less established than their neighbours across the road and the Brown family lived at No. 25 from around 1911–40. The Hinds were at No. 28 for a similar period and others who stayed put for long periods were the Webbs, next door at No. 29, Frederick Payne at No. 31, the Wells at No. 33, and George Jenman at No. 38. Silas Wilkins lived at No. 39 from around 1887–1931 and the Edsall family were at No. 43 between the two world wars. William Jacobs was at No. 44 for four decades as was Joseph Elkins at No. 46. Edward Major was a dock boatman for the London & South Western Railway and lived at No. 51 from around 1911–40.

Although the street numbers ended at 53, a No. 54 was shown in the directory of 1887 but this was renumbered as No. 1 Deal Street, next to the Dock Tavern

*Looking north up Dock Street with St Mary's Mission Room in the distance (Southampton City Archive).*

*A party in Dock Street in the 1930s, possibly celebrating the 1936 Coronation (Courtesy Ted Beard).*

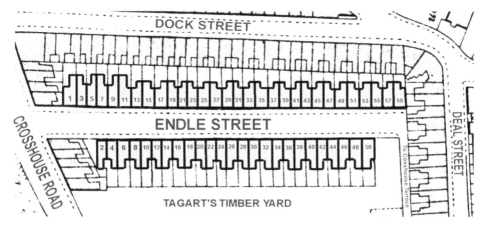

*Endle Street in 1910, showing the full allocation of street numbers up to No. 59 but the even numbers stopped at 50.*

## ENDLE STREET

Originally named River Street, Endle Street ran north to south, parallel with Dock Street. At its northern end was a passage leading along the back of Deal Street to Crosshouse Terrace. River Street did not appear in the street directories until 1891, and then it was

*Air raid shelters amid a scene of devastation in Endle Street after the World War Two bombing raids (Southampton City Archive).*

only the east side, Nos. 2–50, but the west side, Nos. 1–59, appeared in the 1901 directory, though there is no record of Nos. 52, 54, 56 and 58. The residents were mainly labourers and dock workers with a few seamen. No. 51 was a shop run by William Adams from the early 1900s until the street was lost in the 1940s. In fact, many of the families were living there continuously for similar periods. Endle Street fared no better than its neighbours during the wartime bombing. It was so badly damaged the whole street was cleared away.

## CROSSHOUSE

Crosshouse, on the west bank of the River Itchen, takes its name from the stone shelter where travellers would wait for the ferry to row them across the river to Itchen Village long before the Floating Bridge came into being. The old Itchen ferry ran from mediaeval times and the shelter still exists today, with its stone walls and conical roof. Nearby were several industries, including sawmills and shipbuilders. Crosshouse Road ran from Floating Bridge Road down to the shore and had several houses and a couple of pubs along its route, with a section known as Crosshouse Terrace down near the old monument.

*The Crosshouse shelter pictured in the 1930s. George Napier & Sons engineering works on the left had closed in the early 1900s. Tagart's sawmill is on the far right (Dave Marden Collection).*

*A summer day on the River Itchen at Crosshouse, with local children paddling amongst the barges and the village of Itchen Ferry on the far shore (Dave Marden Collection).*

Almost everything in this area was destroyed in the war but, in the years afterwards, Crosshouse was a meeting place for many of Chapel's old boys, who swapped yarns and tended their boats, some of which very occasionally went out onto the water. Names that immediately come to mind are Harry Bray, Gussie Woodford and Jackie Knapp. In those days, you could lay down a mooring with a rope tied to a piece of masonry with a float and nobody would bother you, but eventually the Harbour Authorities realised there was money in this and you had to have a mooring licence. These grew increasingly expensive and local residents' boats remained on dry land.

## CROSSHOUSE TERRACE

For many years, Crosshouse was almost a separate community from Chapel itself, with a collection of houses at Crosshouse Terrace that had been occupied since at least the 1830s, much earlier than those in Crosshouse Road. In amongst the buildings of this hamlet were The Ship and the White Swan, both of which, like most of their neighbours, had disappeared in the wartime bombing which was aimed at the Supermarine Works on the opposite side of the River Itchen. Not much has come to light about The Ship in my research, other than the fact that it appears in the 1851 street directory, run by beer retailer Mrs Elizabeth Andrews. Thomas Andrews, an anchor blacksmith, had been in residence at Crosshouse since the 1830s and died in 1850. It would appear this was his

*The Garibaldi Arms in happier times, with locals perhaps ready for an outing in their Sunday best. The carriage was supplied by Percy Nash of 20 Orchard Lane (Peter Wardall Collection).*

*Crosshouse Road showing its two pubs with the Garibaldi Arms (GA) on the corner of Dock Street and the White Swan (WS) near the Crosshouse shelter. No location of the Ship has yet come to light but it was possibly at No. 2 Crosshouse Terrace.*

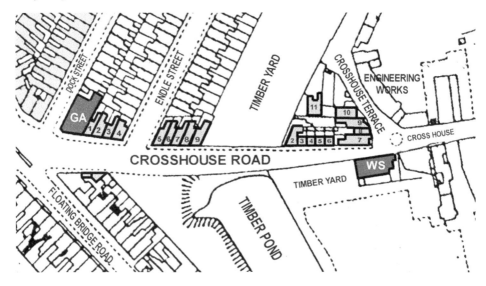

wife making a living to support their six children. As to its location, it may have been at No. 2 Crosshouse Terrace, which was later a shop.

The White Swan stood on the east side of the road, adjacent to the old shelter. It dated back to the early 1800s, when Thomas Dear was the landlord. Local shipbuilder and later celebrated politician, John Ransom (see *Albert Road – Ransom's Terrace*) was proprietor in the 1820s and owner for several decades. Cooper's Brewery were the owners by 1933 when the pub was refused a licence but it continued to appear in the street directories up to 1940, when it presumably met the same fate as all the neighbouring properties.

Crosshouse Terrace was a strange triangular collection of buildings where the house numbers were a little haphazard. At the other side of Crosshouse Terrace stood a shipbuilding and repair yard, then down on Crosshouse Wharf were a number of businesses including Richard Westlake's sack factory and Tagart, Morgan & Coles' steam-driven sawmill.

## CROSSHOUSE ROAD

On the west side of the street the Garibaldi Arms stood on the corner of Crosshouse Road and Dock Street. It was recorded back in 1871 as the Garibaldi Inn, being part of what was then Garibaldi Terrace, named after Giuseppe Garibaldi, the Italian military patriot. Dating from the 1860s, the pub belonged to Panton's Wareham Brewery until 1892 when taken over by Scrace's Star Brewery, who then owned the pub until it was sold again, this time to Strong's of Romsey in the 1920s. Benjamin Living, an engineer by trade, was landlord from the 1880s until at least 1925. Leonard Stote then took over and ran the pub until 1940.

For generations after World War Two, people still spoke of 'The night the Garibaldi got hit', this being one of the more terrible tragedies of the Blitz. In November 1940, all its customers, including several sailors, were killed when the building received a direct hit. Mrs and Mrs Reynolds, who had only taken charge of the pub some two weeks previously, also perished, but, miraculously, their four children survived by sheltering under the bar. The site is now occupied by commercial premises.

Next to the pub was a terrace of four houses (Nos. 1–4) which continued after Endle Street as Nos. 5–9. Next was a large timber yard that stretched all the way back to Deal

Street before the next huddle of houses that were down by the Crosshouse shelter. These were at the eastern end of Crosshouse Terrace, which ran from Elm Road near the corporation yard.

There was little else on the east side of Crosshouse Road, running back to Floating Bridge Road, save for a timber pond with sheds and a couple of houses, Nos. 1A and 1B, that were tucked beside the fried fish shop on the corner of the street. There was also a Crosshouse Cottage, occupied from 1914–40 by John William Budden, but I have yet to locate its whereabouts.

# CHAPTER 10.

## The Docks Area

The area down by the docks may or may not be construed as Chapel, but it was part of the downtown neighbourhood which housed so many people employed in the docks and shipping. This was a mixture of older and newer places where the later streets of Chapel met the older docks district. This chapter includes everything south of Chantry Road with Royal Crescent Road, Lower Bridge Road and Guillaume Terrace, together with Canute Road running down to the Floating Bridge.

### ROYAL CRESCENT ROAD

Royal Crescent Road was another of those thoroughfares that developed piecemeal from small groups of buildings and, in this case, from two streets. It was originally made up of two separate parts. The first, known as just Royal Crescent, ran from Canute Road to Lower Bridge Road, while the section named Royal Crescent Road ran from Lower Bridge Road to Chantry Road (the part that passed under the Central Bridge). The two merged into one during the 1920s, which also saw the various buildings renumbered.

On the west side, the Canute Castle Hotel was included in the Crescent in early directories but soon became listed in Canute Road. The adjacent buildings in Royal Crescent were numbered 1–7 and consisted mainly of hotels, eateries and coffee houses. Under the

*Royal Crescent Road in 1910, showing the entire length and the cluster of commercial premises at the Canute Road end that formed the original Royal Crescent. Tram lines are shown on the Central Bridge which crosses the site.*

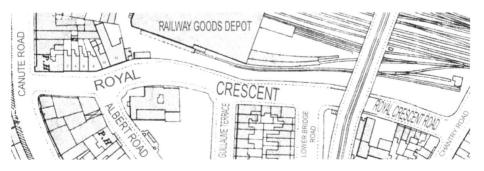

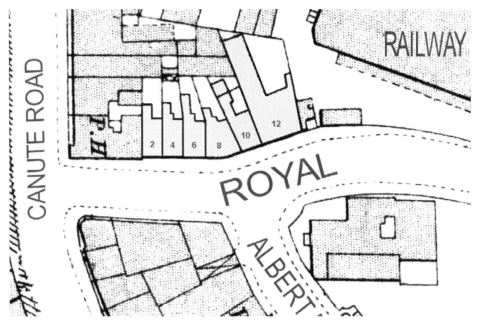

*A closer look at the southern end of Royal Crescent west side, where hotels and eating houses beckoned customers from the docks. The site was for many later years occupied by the Walkers Packing Company building erected in the 1960s.*

renumbering scheme in the 1920s these became even Nos. 2–12 with odd numbers on the opposite side of the road.

Under the old numbering system, No. 1 was the Crescent Hotel from the 1870s until closure in 1915. It then became a tobacconist, before Mrs Annie Hampton opened her dining rooms there in the 1920s and the premises remained as such until the 1960s, when it became Charles Malizia's betting shop.

In 1881, the old No. 2 was shown as the Coffee Tavern and shortly afterwards as the Dock Cocoa Tavern, but by the late 1880s it had become the Workman's Institute and Dining Rooms, afterwards dropping the 'institute' and becoming just plain dining rooms from the turn of the century. They were run by the Kennedy family for a decade before they were destroyed by wartime bombing in 1940.

The next few premises are somewhat confusing as, next door, the old No. 3 was William Baker's grocery and wine merchants store in the 1880s before becoming Baker & Co. Outfitters aground the turn of the century; the shop then became absorbed into the

Cyprus Hotel at No. 4, which was previously named the Rosen Hotel. However, the 1863 directory lists Nos. 3 and 4 as the Hotel de Providence run by one Madame C. Houillon, but this may have been a reference to the Providence Hotel at the adjacent No. 2 St Lawrence Road which, in 1911, was run by Emile Gorlanti while accommodating emigrants awaiting voyage on the White Star Line ships to America.

No. 5 was the Lord Nelson Hotel dating from the 1860s until its closure in 1933, and appears to have remained empty after that until destroyed with its neighbours in World War Two. Likewise, No. 6, which was the Bee Hive Inn from the same decade, until being renamed, firstly as the Bee Hive Hotel in the 1880s and then the Florence Hotel at the turn of the century.

This line of buildings, originally Nos. 1–6, became Nos. 2–12 in the 1920s renumbering scheme, after which, as the new No. 2, the Hampton Dining Rooms became the only building of the row to survive the Blitz. The remainder of the west side of Royal Crescent,

*A post-World War Two view of the southern end of Royal Crescent Road, showing Mrs Annie Hampton's dining rooms next to the Canute Castle Hotel. The empty space in the foreground is the site of the former Bell Brothers warehouse destroyed by bombing (Dave Marden Collection).*

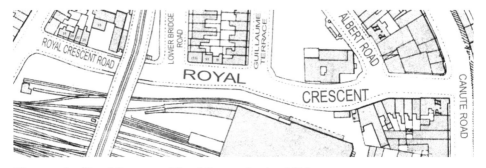

*The east side of Royal Crescent and Royal Crescent Road in 1910.*

all the way along to Chantry Road, was the boundary of the London & South Western Railway goods depot.

Continuing with the original numbering system, Nos. 7 and 8 were on the east side of the street between Guillaume Terrace and Lower Bridge Road. From the early 1900s, No. 7 became coffee rooms run by the Gibbs family and No. 8 is shown as Dolman's Dining Rooms back in 1916. No. 9 was Bell Brothers Ships Stores, occupying a warehouse on the corner of Albert Road. Adjoining this building, towards Canute Road around 1890, was a Customs House which from the turn of the century became temporary barracks for troops embarking for overseas duties. It was afterwards known as the Minden Receiving Depot until becoming the Royal Army Ordnance Corps stores depot about 1930.

*A closer view of the east side of Royal Crescent with Nos. 9, 11 and 13 between Guillaume Terrace and Lower Bridge Road. No. 10 was the Seamen's Mission standing on the Mead recreation ground. The building on the corner of Albert Road was Bell Brothers Stores which once was No. 9 in an early scheme.*

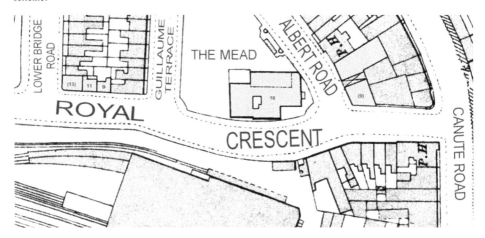

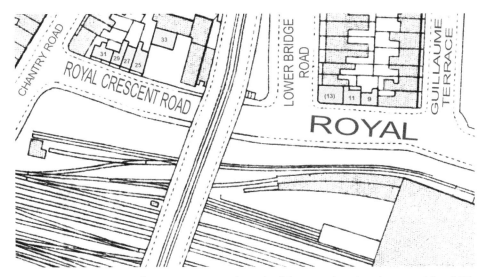

Buildings on the east side of Royal Crescent Road, north of the Central Bridge where Nos. 25 and 37 were once cottages with names and No. 31 was formerly two houses.

Royal Crescent Road looking north towards the Central Bridge with the Southampton Terminus Goods Depot on the left. To the right stands No. 17 Guillaume Terrace, with Nos. 9 and 11 Royal Crescent Road behind it and the Rose, Shamrock & Thistle pub just visible on the corner of Lower Bridge Road. The scene is a publicity photo showing Glaxo Red Cross parcels being loaded for delivery to the Royal Victoria Hospital at Netley (Dave Marden Collection).

No. 10 was the Waterside Mission Hall back in 1884. This building occupied a prominent position on a recreation ground known as The Mead. By the 1900s it had become the Missions to Seamen, and had acquired an attached coffee room by 1912. In later years this became an annex to Deanery School before the site was finally cleared and the former recreation ground given over to commercial premises such as Southern Auto Parks. The area was again transformed in the 1970s, with construction of the Itchen Bridge and the new Saltmarsh Road. The Aviation Museum 'Solent Sky' now stands roughly in its place.

Further along Royal Crescent Road, north of the Central Bridge was a collection of buildings numbered 1–5 near Chantry Road. Back in 1863 there is reference to Royal Crescent Cottages, where No. 1 was a boarding house run by Elizabeth Bamburgh and No. 2 was occupied by mariner Richard Wood. These may well have been the same two buildings that were later named Laura Cottage and Agnes Cottage in 1881. Nos. 3–5 was a small terrace where 4 and 5 appear to have been combined as one building in the 1880s.

These buildings took the numbers 25–31 in the revised scheme while the old Nos 7 and 8 became 9 and 11 with the Rose Shamrock & Thistle pub, on the corner of Lower Bridge Road, becoming No. 13. There was also a No. 33 which was a yard adjacent to Central Bridge which, from the 1930s to 1960s, belonged to paint manufacturer Robert Ingham Clarke & Co.

## GUILLAUME TERRACE

Guillaume Terrace took its name from George Guillaume, who was the corporation's surveyor from 1846 and oversaw the development of the old salt marsh, which became part of the lower Chapel area. The terrace was cleared away in the 1970s during the construction of the Itchen Bridge.

Facing the open expanse of The Mead recreation ground, the houses along Guillaume Terrace must have been desirable properties when built. Most were three storeys and several were at one time lodging houses. Nos. 7, 9, 10, 11, 12, 15 and 17 were all listed as such at various times from the 1800s to the 1920s.

No. 1 was originally a shop run by George Goddard from the 1860s until the 1880s. In 1912, No. 2 became the headquarters of the Dock, Wharf, Riverside & General Workers'

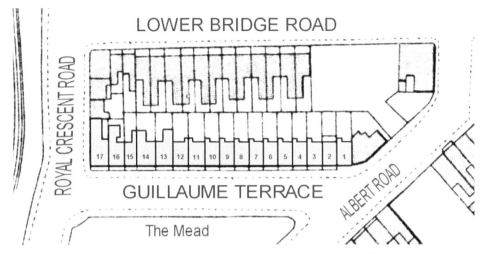

*The once impressive Guillaume Terrace sat between Royal Crescent Road and Albert Road. The building adjacent to No. 1 was once the Saracen's Head pub, which later became the Albert Stores (see Albert Road).*

Union, whose district organiser and secretary was one William Paul, until the 1920s when the Carter family moved in.

The Lee family lived at No. 5 from the turn of the century until the mid-1930s and Benjamin Hills moved into No. 9 during World War One and stayed until the 1950s, likewise the Ede family were at No. 15 for the same period. Miss Maude Simmons resided in No. 10 from the 1920s until the mid-1950s when Nos. 1–12 were demolished and part of the site was taken over by a row of garages in the 1960s.

Nos. 13–17 remained in place until the rest of the terrace came down in the late 1960s, with the Wort family being one of the final street residents at No. 13, and one of the longer stays was that of the Middlewicks at No. 14 from pre-World War Two until the very end.

On a couple of occasions, a No. 16A appeared in the directories, firstly in 1940 and again in the 1960s. This may have referred to an annexe at the rear, or perhaps the house was divided.

# LOWER BRIDGE ROAD

Lower Bridge Road ran from Royal Crescent Road to Canute Road. It was once a continuation of Bridge Street (now Bernard Street) across the other side of the main railway line to the Terminus Station. The road also incorporated Bridge Terrace, a section between

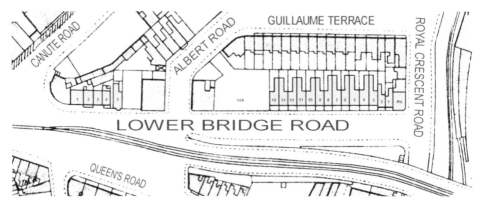

*Nos. 1–5 Bridge Terrace stood between the Marsh Hotel on the corner of Canute Road and the Royal Albert Hotel at the junction with Albert Road. The York & Albany pub stood opposite. Lower Bridge Road was alongside the Central Bridge, shown here with its tram lines. The Rose, Shamrock & Thistle pub stood on the corner of Royal Crescent Road and, with the two houses next to it (Nos. 1 and 2), were the three original buildings, the others (Nos. 1–14) not being built until 1900.*

Canute Road and Albert Road, where much of it still stands between the former Marsh and Royal Albert Hotels.

Bridge Terrace stood opposite the former Queen's Road (see Chantry Road) and was in evidence long becoming absorbed by Lower Bridge Road. It is an interesting line of buildings, most of which still stand to this day.

No. 1 was a ship's chandlery and baker's in the early 1900s run by George Beach, and by 1914 it had become a newsagent's and post office which also included a telephone call office. Pre-World War Two it was a confectioner's run by James Long, and after the war it became the Popular Café until the 1960s when it was a Transport Café. No. 2 was always a residence while No. 3 was a baker's, greengrocer's and, for a while, a ladies' hairdresser's in the 1960s before becoming the Crusty Cottage Bakery in the 1970s.

No. 4 was a residence but No. 5 was another commercial premises, being a grocer's run by William Saunders in the early 1900s. For a while, either side of World War Two, it incorporated a post office. By the 1960s it was taken over by general dealer Bernard McEvoy.

In 1897, Lower Bridge Road consisted of just three buildings, these being the Rose, Shamrock & Thistle pub (at other times listed as No. 13 Royal Crescent Road) and the adjacent Lorne Villas which were a couple of large houses next door to the pub. The villas were substantial three-storey houses like those behind them in Guillaume Terrace. The rest

*Lower Bridge Road viewed from Central Bridge with the Rose, Shamrock &Thistle pub on the corner of Royal Crescent Road and the two LorneVillas (houses Nos. 1 and 2) next door as pictured in 1968 (Dave Marden).*

*A closer view of the Shamrock in its days as a Brickwoods house (Dave Goddard Collection).*

*Looking west at Bridge Terrace towards the Central Bridge in 1968, with the Marsh Hotel on the extreme left. The Royal Albert and the York & Albany pubs are in the centre with Lower Bridge Road in the distance. This street area is now completely obliterated by the Itchen Bridge (Dave Marden).*

of the street, Nos. 1–14, wasn't built until 1900 and one of the houses bore a stone tablet to proclaim this. These were some of the last houses built in the downtown area, and also among the last to be cleared during the construction of the Itchen Bridge. There was also a No. 14A adjacent to the York and Albany pub which was a yard and store. During the 1960s and 1970s this was occupied by electrical contractors F. W. Cook & Co.

The Rose, Shamrock & Thistle dated back to the 1870s when the landlord was John Player. From the early 1900s until the 1920s, Origen Hoffman was in charge when the pub was owned Barlow's Victorian Brewery, and the 1930s and 1940s saw Charles Bennett behind the bar. It was a Brickwoods house by the time it ceased trading in November 1968, and its site was later lost under the Itchen Bridge development.

## FLOATING BRIDGE ROAD

Floating Bridge Road was just that – the road to the Floating Bridge which was a ferry that ran from just south of Crosshouse across the River Itchen to Woolston. The Floating Bridge

*An 1840 engraving of the rather grand Floating Bridge Toll House, which straddled the road on approach to the ferry. This view looks east towards the ferry which can be glimpsed through the centre archway (Dave Marden Collection).*

ferry first appeared in 1836 as competition to the Toll Bridge at Northam, and ran until it was replaced by Itchen Bridge in 1977. The ferry company also built roads on either side of the River Itchen to accommodate traffic, one of these was Albert Road which linked Floating Bridge Road to the wharves at Marine Parade.

Floating Bridge Road itself formed part of the original route from the town to the ferry that included Bridge Terrace, Lower Bridge Road and Bernard Street (formerly Bridge Street). From the beginning, the ferry company had a large and ornate Toll House which straddled the road to the ferry, the central section was eventually removed and one of the outer buildings on the north side was still evident in the 1950s. The tolls were dispensed with when the corporation bought out the ferry company in 1934. The ferry itself was steam-powered for most of its life until diesel-driven vessels took over in 1962, lasting until the Itchen Bridge was opened in 1977.

The road had odd numbers 1–45 on its northern side. No. 1 was variously a grocer's shop and refreshment rooms until becoming a fried fish shop around 1900. Miss Florence Smith ran it from the First World War until the mid-1920s. After

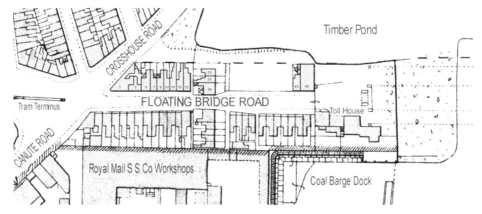

*The north side of Floating Bridge Road in 1910, with odd Nos. 1—45. By then, the original toll house (part of which was No. 19) was replaced with an office nearer to the ferry.*

several changes of ownership, Frederick Lawrence took over in the 1930s until, like several of its neighbours, the building was destroyed by bombs in World War Two.

No. 3 had been a sweet shop since the 1920s but was taken over by Roy Staples as a pie shop in the late 1930s. When that was destroyed in the war he moved his pie

*A fine study of Floating Bridge No. 8 in the early 1900s. The last floating bridge made its way across the River Itchen on 11 June 1977. As one who was born and brought up in the Chapel area of Southampton, I felt privileged to have this marvellous mode of transport on my doorstep and made full use of it — especially as it was free to pedestrians and cyclists in my day. It is now 40 years since that final trip took place (Dave Marden Collection).*

*No. 19 Floating Bridge Road was once part of the original Toll House which spanned the street from 1836, and is pictured here in 1933. It remained in place as a residence until the 1950s and No. 21 is shown next to it, on the right (Southampton City Archive).*

shop to No. 7, which had also previously been a sweet shop from the early 1900s, but after the war it became a grocer's shop until the 1960s when it went back to being a bakery and became one of last buildings to survive until the 1970s.

Mrs Fuller ran No. 11 as apartments and lived there from around 1914–40, then William Marshall moved in post-war and remained in residence until that part of the street was taken down in the 1960s. No. 17 was also a tobacconist's and confectioner's shop through the 1960s.

No. 19 had an interesting history as it formed part of the original Ferry Company Toll House erected in 1836 and, with its neighbour across the road (No. 28), it

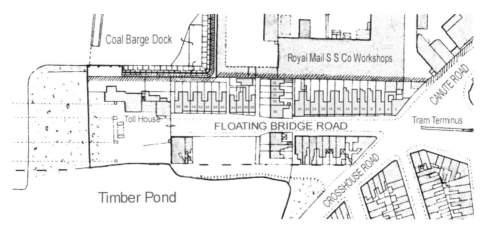

*The south side of Floating Bridge Road in 1910 where the houses, odd Nos. 2–58 backed on to the docks boundary wall. As with its neighbour across the street at No. 19, No. 28 was once part of the original toll house dating from 1836.*

spanned the street until the centre section was demolished and they became two separate houses. In the 1880s it was known as Bridge House and was occupied by the superintendent of the ferry company. Meanwhile, the toll collection point was moved to a new building nearer the ferry, which remained in action until the 1930s when tolls were removed after the Corporation bought out the Floating Bridge Company and ran it until closure.

No. 45, adjacent to the ferry, was the premises of the Hellyer family who were woodcarvers in the 1880s, and by the early 1900s it was taken over by sail makers Beaton Brothers who were there until the bombs fell in 1940.

A similar fate befell No. 2 on the south side of the street. Standing on the corner of Canute Road it had been a clothier's during the 1880s, and from the early 1900s it was coffee rooms until about 1930, when it became, briefly, a musical warehouse. In the years immediately prior to World War Two it had been used as dining rooms, only to be lost to the bombing. The Early family also lived at that address from the 1900s until 1940. After the war, the building was resurrected as No. 2A and became a sub-post office under J. R. Baldwyn until the 1960s, when G. A. Mills took over and also ran a newsagent's there.

Nos. 2A–24 largely survived the war and lasted until 1970 when the much of the street came down, leaving only Nos. 46–48 remaining until they too were cleared to make way for the Itchen Bridge. No. 4 was, at various times in the 1950s, a chemist and a fishmonger's, and finally a general shop run by R. S. Davis.

*Looking towards Floating Bridge Road with a tram at the Bridge Terrace terminus. The shops and houses on the left of the picture were all badly damaged beyond repair in World War Two while the sub-Post Office can be seen on the corner of Canute Road to the right of the tram (Peter Wardall Collection).*

*A post-war view looking east towards Floating Bridge Road after the bus routes were extended to the Floating Bridge Hard. The buildings to the immediate left of the tram are at the end of Crosshouse Road (Dave Marden Collection).*

No. 8 was home to the Sweet family from the early 1900s until it was taken over by Johnson & Frederick as a tobacconist and confectionery after World War Two. They also had the next-door premises at No. 10, which had previously been a general shop run by Mrs R. DeBeaucamp from the early 20th century until William Parker took over in the 1920s and turned it into a sweet shop. Johnson & Frederick kept the shop going until the 1960s, when No. 8 became Bert Carlisle's betting shop and No. 10 became a café under several ownerships until 1970.

Another general shop was No. 12, run by Mrs Elizabeth King from the First World War until the 1940s. After the Second World War, William Hooper moved in and stayed through the final years of the street until 1970. No. 14 also had long-term residents, with Miss Haynes living there from the early 1900s until Miss Lee took over after World War Two and stayed to the end in 1970.

Floating Bridge Road was also the terminus of the tram service which stopped well short of the ferry at the junction with Canute Road. It wasn't until after 1950 that the replacement bus route was extended to nearer the ferry landing.

## CANUTE ROAD

Although not strictly within the confines of 'Chapel', Canute Road is included due to its importance to the area. The route of this thoroughfare was once just a rough causeway separating the mudflats of the river from the marshlands that came to be Chapel. It must have been a very wild and desolate place and some old maps show an Admiralty gallows there, possibly for the hanging of pirates.

The area was totally transformed with the arrival of the London & Southampton Railway together with the building of the docks, either side of 1840. After that the area boomed with hotels, cafés, pubs, shipping company offices and the many streets of houses that became homes to the workforce that served the docks and sailed on the ships. This all led to the creation of latter-day Chapel, which rapidly grew through to the 1870s. For the purposes of this book I will refer only to the properties on the north side of the road as I regard those opposite to be part of, or particular to, the Docks.

Initially, Canute Road extended only from the South Western Hotel to Royal Crescent Road. The section east of Royal Crescent, towards the Floating Bridge, was known as Oriental Place due to the imposing Oriental Buildings that stood opposite the Canute Dock gate. These were the offices of the Peninsular & Oriental Steam Navigation Company (P&O) and also provided overnight accommodation for its officers.

The early horse-drawn trams ran along Canute Road to the Floating Bridge from 1879, but were then diverted over the Central Bridge from 1901.

The South Western Hotel began life as the Imperial Hotel in 1865 and was purchased by the London & South Western Railway Company in 1871. It served as accommodation for passengers travelling on the ocean liners until 1939, when it was taken over by the military during the war years. Afterwards, it housed the offices of the Cunard Shipping Company and then the television studios of BBC South, before becoming converted into apartments from 1997–99.

The buildings along the north side of Canute Road between St Lawrence Road and Royal Crescent have been mainly commercial premises since the time they were built in the 1850s, and renumbered several times during their existence.

On the corner of St Lawrence Road stands a building that was originally the New York Hotel, built in 1851, its early landlord was Joseph Dogget. He was succeeded in the 1860s by Thomas Mead but the hotel seems to have gone out of business by the next decade. It was taken over by the railway in 1894 and became known as South Western Chambers in 1897.

*Canute Road in 1910 with buildings on the north side highlighted, running from the South Western Hotel at one end to the Marsh Hotel at the other.*

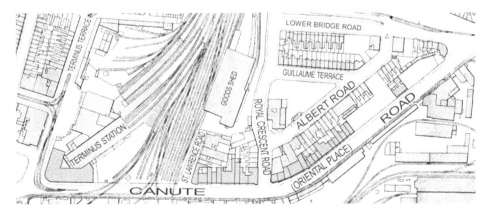

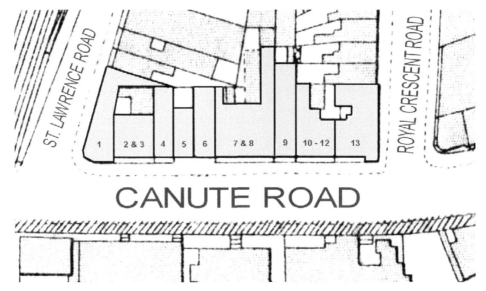

*The section of Canute Road between St Lawrence Road and Royal Crescent Road showing Nos. 1–13 on the north side around 1910. The numbers and buildings changed over the years.*

It was previously not numbered, but became No. 1 around the 1950s. Having once housed the Chamber of Commerce before the First World War, then from the 1920s it became home to a number of meat company offices until the outbreak of World War Two, after which it became the offices of various British Railways departments until the 1960s when radar specialists Halpins of Hampshire moved in. In the 1970s several commercial firms shared the building, including bookmaker Charles Malizia, later taken over by Ladbrokes, on the ground floor. It is currently the offices of an estate agency.

Nos. 2 and 3 Canute Road appear to be one building served by a number of entrances. No. 2 was once one of several premises run by Miller & Co. who were outfitters there in the 1870s until the turn of the century. At that time Hughes & Co. ran a chemist shop at No. 3, but later moved into No. 2 where John Hughes also set up as a dentist. The chemist's shop was eventually taken over by Bates & Co. in the 1920s. After the late 1930s the building became home to several shipping agencies and after World War Two it was occupied by a couple of printing firms until the 1970s. Millers also occupied Nos. 3 and 4 in the 1880s, until Cumming & Co.'s ships chandlers moved in prior to World War One, thereafter several shipping agency firms have been there.

No. 5 began life as the Ship Tavern back in the 1850s under landlord Thomas McLorinan, and then saw a succession of licensees until it closed in 1933 when owned by Aldridge's Bedford Brewery. Although sustaining wartime damage, it then carried on as refreshment rooms and a café under several ownerships, trading for many years as Toni's Snack Bar. It is now a Chinese takeaway.

No. 6 was another outlet for Millers outfitters from the 1850s to around 1912, when it became home to shipping agents before being lost in the wartime bombing.

Nos. 7 and 8 was a building housing the officers' accommodation for the Royal Mail Steam Packet Company until the early 1900s, when taken over by the Board of Trade. The White Star Line moved in during the 1920s and 1930s when part of the accommodation became the Atlantic Café. The buildings were destroyed during the war and subsequently became the home of the BTC Sports & Social Club until more recently replaced by an apartment block.

During the 1870s and 1880s, building No. 9 was the premises of Joseph Stebbing, a nautical instrument maker who also had an observatory there with views over the docks and down Southampton Water. In the 20th century it became a ships chandler and eventually became part of the site redeveloped for the BTC Club.

Nos. 10, 11 and 12 appear to be part of one building adjacent to the Canute Castle Hotel. In the early 1900s, No. 10 was occupied by money changer Robert Gerth until the 1920s, when Stephen Lodge ran a stationers there when it became Denton's tobacconists after World War Two and the premises was latterly a café. Lodge also ran a hairdresser's at No. 12 until around 1960, when T. Johnson took over until the 1970s. The rest of the building was taken up by various port-related businesses.

No. 13 was the Canute Castle Hotel from the 1850s, when it also contained a billiard room. It was run by Thomas Phillips and also by builder Sam Stevens in its early years. By the 1880s, the Awberry family ran the hotel until the 1920s. In the early 1900s it was owned by Perkin's Globe Brewery until taken over by Brickwoods around 1925. Thereafter, the McCarthy family were 'mine hosts' until the post-World War Two years and Whitbreads took over in 1971. The pub traded for 20 more years until the building was found to be unsafe in 1991. After undergoing major repairs, it traded briefly as the Trawler's Bar in

*The Ship Inn was an early dockland pub and once known as a London & Dublin Stout House. Amazingly, those words are still discernable high up on the building (Dave Goddard Collection).*

*A scene from days gone by as horse cabs wait in line for custom at Canute Road. The South Western Hotel at the Terminus Station looms in the background (Dave Marden Collection).*

1993, and the building is now home to an estate agency with the major part being converted to flats.

As previously mentioned, the remainder of the street east of Royal Crescent was originally known as Oriental Place, with the P&O Shipping Company's Oriental Buildings taking pride of place opposite the dock gate. These buildings had a separate numbering system (Nos. 1–4) from the rest of the street that were numbered 1–13 (No. 13 being the Sailors' Home) and later became occupied by various shipping company and agency offices. Much of this area was heavily bombed in the Second World War and very few of the original buildings survived.

Under the street renumbering scheme, the buildings became Nos. 14–34 (34 being the Sailors' Home). No. 14 was, in the 1880s, a grocer's shop and run by a Mr Godden, while No. 15 was the Coffee Tavern and Temperance Restaurant run by John Doling, who was later in charge of the Emigrants (Atlantic) Hotel in Albert Road. Both 14 and 15 later became used by port-related companies from the turn of the century.

Nos. 16–19 was the site of the aforementioned Oriental Buildings and was taken over by a host of users. By the turn of the 20th century, No. 16 was occupied by outfitters Baker & Co., together with hairdresser Basil Collins and the Wilts & Dorset Bank. No. 17 was used by a host of shipping company agents as well as a tobacconist's shop run by Sidney Hampton and afterwards by Alfred Davies in the 1930s to 1940, when destroyed by bombing. This part of the street was rebuilt in the 1960s and used mainly by ships store merchants.

Nos. 18 and 19, the main part of the former Oriental Buildings, became the home of several anti-fouling paint companies, together with the usual plethora of shipping agents

*The section of Canute Road east of Royal Crescent where Nos. 16–19 were the site of the Oriental Chambers.*

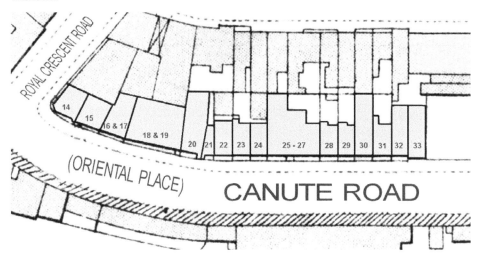

until the bombs took their toll. After the war, the buildings were replaced by those of several companies, amongst them British Ropes and the seamen's registry of the Shipping Federation, both of which lasted into the 1970s.

No. 20 (formerly No. 3) was once the offices of Lloyds Register of Shipping from the turn of the century until the 1920s, while Nos. 21–24 held yet more shipping company agencies' offices.

Nos. 25–27 formed the Dock Hotel, another hostelry dating back to the 1850s when Henry Morgan was the proprietor. It was also known as the Hotel Francais at one time. George Hoffman was in charge from the 1880s to the early 1900s, with R. G. Butson being the final licensee when bombs fell in the Second World War.

No. 28 at one time housed Lloyds Register of Shipping in the 1880s and then the usual smattering of shipping agencies before being taken over by the firm of International Paints, along with Nos. 29 and 30, in the 1950s until recent years. No. 30 was also used by Frank Livett ships stores in the 1960s. No. 31 was home to the London & North Western Railway Company officers from the 1870s until World War One, after which it seems to have been

*The Marsh Hotel in later years under the shadow of the Itchen Bridge (Dave Goddard Collection).*

*An engraving of Oriental Buildings around 1851 with the tower of the Canute Castle Hotel in the background at the entrance to Royal Crescent Road (Dave Marden Collection).*

*An old illustration of Oriental Place drawn by Philip Brannon in the 1850s. The Dock Hotel had opened around that time. This later became part of Canute Road with the hotel being numbered 25/27 (Dave Marden Collection).*

unused (or possibly renumbered) until the 1960s, when taken over by the ship stores companies of E. Buckle & Sons and Vernon & Tear. No. 32 was also used by Vernon & Tear in the 1960s.

No. 33 was the Gough Ice & Cold Storage premises from the 1920s until the 1960s, when a number of meat and frozen food companies took over. Also in the 1960s part of the building became the Key Club which, after closure, reopened in 1981 as the Frog & Frigate pub and is one of the few original buildings left in that part of the street. Nos. 34–36 are relatively new buildings, dating from the 1960s and mainly operated as ships stores and cold stores.

For many years there was open ground along the rest of the north side of Canute Road between No. 34 and the Marsh Hotel at No. 42. The Marsh, named after the area it stood in, is recorded in 1871 as being run by John Molson under the ownership of Cooper's Brewery. Henry Elliot was a long-serving licensee there from the early 1900s until the mid-1930s, when the Norman family took charge until the 1950s. Having served a spell under Watney's it became a Marston pub in 1957. The pub closed in 2002 but the building survives and is now converted into flats.

More flats eventually filled the space next to the Marsh when the Utility Flats were built in the 1930s. They numbered 3–30 but oddly, there was no 11 or 12, nor 21 or 22. The buildings were renovated and modernised during the 1980s when the nearby Outer Dock became Ocean Village.

## ST LAWRENCE ROAD

Although St Lawrence Road was not strictly in the Chapel area, like Canute Road it was on the fringes and has been included. The road itself was little more than a cul-de-sac leading from Canute Road to the LSWR's yard and goods shed adjacent to the Terminus Station, but at one time it housed several commercial premises, hotels and a pub in the early boom period following the arrival of the railway and the building of the docks. Early incumbents were the LSWR's telegraph offices and the Royal Mail Shipping Company Stores.

At No. 2, next door to the New York Hotel (see *Canute Road*), was the Eagle Tavern which appears to have been one of the earlier pubs near the docks dating from the 1850s, with landlady Elizabeth Berry, but the enterprise was fairly brief as the pub had disappeared by the 1870s and become LSWR offices.

*St Lawrence Road showing Nos. 2–7 along its eastern side where several hostelries sprang up following the arrival of the railway.*

*A view of Canute Road taken from the South Western Hotel looking east towards the River Itchen. St Lawrence Road is on the left behind the railway sidings with the former New York Hotel prominent on its corner (Dave Marden Collection).*

The St Lawrence Hotel at No. 3 fared little better than its next-door neighbour, the Eagle Tavern. Having been run by Henry Cole (Beer Retailer and Eating House Keeper) in the early 1850s and 1860s, it was taken over by William Compton during the late 1860s but had closed in the early 1870s, also being taken over by the LSWR to become its telegraph offices.

From around 1850 the Providence Hotel at Nos. 5–7 was run by Patrick Crowley and had Madame C. Houillon as proprietor in the 1860s, but by the 1870s it was owned by one Madame Josephine Toussaint and was then known as the Hotel de la Providence, when it appears to have catered for a mainly French clientele. Madame Toussaint reined supreme until around 1914, when the hotel was taken over by Madame J. E. Pagella. Following several more changes of ownership, the hotel was run by Harry Shaddick in the late 1930s until it was destroyed in wartime bombing.